KNITTING
More
CIRCLES
AROUND SOCKS

Two at a Time, Toe Up or Cuff Down

ANTJE GILLINGHAM

DEDICATION

To my most special Super Love, once again you have shown amazing patience and stood by me with steadfast strength and guidance. Thank you for being my husband, my love, my life.

ACKNOWLEDGMENTS

To merely say thank you to the following highly talented sock knitters seems insufficient gratitude for all the hard work and all the help they've given me over the past few months, but it is all I have to give. Kerma Bowman, Malinda Conger, Amanda Gibson, Laurie Holmes, Stephanie McManus, and Carol O'Connor: ladies, please accept my humble thank-you. I could have never pulled it off without your patience and support.

Thank you to Martingale & Company for believing in me and my socks, especially Ursula Reikes who continues to work hard at creating a knitting book with the highest standards.

Special thanks to my friend Maryann Brown, who once again tested pattern after pattern with a hawk's eye, and who with her amazing number skills saved many a pattern from certain mathematical doom.

Knitting More Circles around Socks:
Two at a Time, Toe Up or Cuff Down
© 2009 by Antje Gillingham

Martingale®
& C O M P A N Y

Martingale & Company
20205 144th Ave. NE
Woodinville, WA 98072-8478 USA
www.martingale-pub.com

Credits

President & CEO: Tom Wierzbicki
Editor in Chief: Mary V. Green
Managing Editor: Tina Cook
Technical Editor: Ursula Reikes
Copy Editor: Sheila Chapman Ryan
Design Director: Stan Green
Production Manager: Regina Girard
Illustrator: Robin Strobel
Cover & Text Designer: Stan Green
Photographer: Brent Kane

Mission Statement

Dedicated to providing quality products and service to inspire creativity.

Printed in China
14 13 12 11 10 09 8 7 6 5 4 3 2 1

**Library of Congress Cataloging-in-Publication Data
is available upon request.**

ISBN: 978-1-56477-915-1

CONTENTS

PREFACE

Oh, dear reader, it's about 3:00 a.m. and the house is utterly still; even the cats have finally given up their quest to get my attention and have gone off to sleep. I'm sitting at the kitchen table enjoying a moment of euphoria—the book is done! The samples are labeled, the pictures are numbered, and the patterns are written. It feels much like the night before Christmas when all the presents are finally wrapped and tucked under the tree.

After months and months of preparation, an amazing amount of coffee, and several nervous breakdowns, that instant when everything comes together even though it seemed impossible has finally arrived.

What a year it's been since *Knitting Circles around Socks* was first published. We'd all hoped for success, of course, but nothing prepared us for the amazing response we received from (sock) knitters all over the world! Thank you so much for your lovely letters and emails, filled with kind words and an undeniable excitement about knitting two socks at a time on two circular needles. Please continue to write. I truly appreciate your input and comments.

As if writing a book wasn't enough, we also moved The Knitting Nest, my yarn shop, to a new home.

A beautiful old brick warehouse that had been refurbished some time ago became available. My husband, Terry, and I were hooked the moment we walked into its lofts. The next three months were spent creating a comfortable, breathtaking space, a sanctuary for knitters to come to and relax. It has become a home away from home for many people, some of who have offered to move in alongside the yarn. Hmm. . . .

I hope that this book, like its predecessor, will give you a reprieve from the hectic schedule of everyday life, and you, dear reader, are a friend who has stopped by to see what's new. Come in, visit a while—it's so good to see you. Of course, I'd love to meet you in person, so please do not hesitate to stop by on your travels and say hello.

~Antje

INTRODUCTION

Hand-knitted socks used to be merely popular. Today, the sock-knitting craze has taken on a whole new dimension! There are sock-of-the-month clubs that cluster around particular yarns. Certain colors and patterns can be attained only if one joins the right group, and a place in the world of intricate patterns and gorgeous colors is highly coveted.

And then there are the Sock Wars, the ultimate affair of the truly obsessed. Here you can show your cunning talent and unsurpassed speed because if you don't knit fast enough, you're out—the goal of a Sock War is to finish your socks and mail them to your recipient before socks are sent to you. Circular needles have quickly given us the upper hand—the speed we need to conquer any assignment and efficiently knock off opponent after opponent. Not only did they free us from working with multiple double-pointed needles, they also saved us from the dreaded knitting-the-second-sock syndrome.

The book you're holding takes the evolution of hand-knitted socks to a higher level still! Let it help you explore the basic techniques with many photographs, illustrations, and detailed instructions. It's all you'll ever need from now on to knit two socks at a time on two circular needles. Forget about counting rows and stitches. Forget about finishing one sock only to have to start the exact same one all over again to get a pair. Stop worrying about whether or not you have enough yarn and don't bother fretting over the perfect fit; just try them on as you go.

No matter how you like to knit your socks—cuff down or toe up—the two basic sock patterns will teach you how to do either or both. The basic cuff-down sock begins on page 19 and is followed by three patterns. The basic toe-up sock begins on page 44 and is followed by seven patterns. Try both basic patterns and see which one you prefer. Being able to work both techniques gives you total control over how you'd like any stitch pattern to look on your socks. Some stitch patterns have a definite up or down direction and how you knit them can make a big difference in the look of your socks.

Above all, have an awesome time learning and testing the techniques that will free you once and for all from the ever-present second-sock syndrome. Turn page after page to find beautiful patterns; wiggle your toes and relax. It's a good day to be a sock knitter!

GETTING STARTED

Here, you'll find information about the parts of socks, the importance of knitting a gauge swatch, and sock sizes.

SOCK TERMINOLOGY

The following illustrations should clarify the exact location of the different parts of a sock. The position of the heel flap, heel turn, and gusset differ slightly depending on whether you're knitting from the cuff down or the toe up.

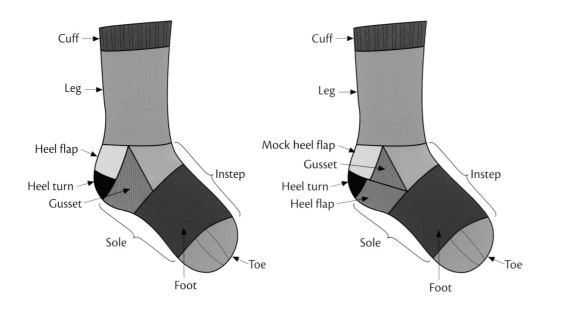

The following illustrations show the measurements that make up a sock.

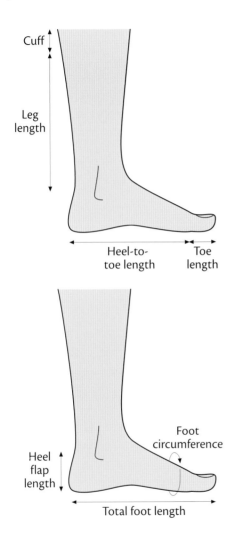

GAUGE

I used to be a very lazy person when it comes to knitting a gauge swatch. But a few knitting disasters taught me to knit a gauge before every project. I drill it into my students as well: knit that gauge if you want your stuff to fit. Sometimes I show them what happens when you don't.

The problem is that we want to start that new project with the gorgeous yarn *now*. But, like flossing your teeth, knitting a gauge is necessary, although tedious. It will assure the correct fit and look of your project, especially if you use expensive or substituted yarn or if you work on, say, two socks simultaneously. The alternative of ripping out all your hard work is even more painful; believe me, I've been there many times. So just bite into that sour apple, knit a swatch, and check those pesky little stitches.

Most patterns tell you to count the stitches over 4". I tell my students to knit the gauge swatch 6" wide and 6" long. If you try to measure the stitches in a 4" x 4" swatch, they will be distorted and incorrect. Always cast on a few more stitches and knit a little longer to be sure that your gauge is accurate.

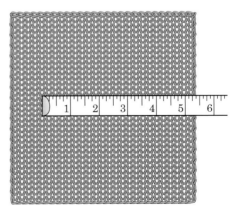

SOCK SIZES

Approximate measurements are provided for children's, women's, and men's sizes. You can alter the size of any sock to fit a child or man by simply casting on a different number of stitches and working the parts of the sock to the appropriate measurements for a given shoe size.

SHOE SIZE	CUFF CIRCUMFERENCE	HEEL-FLAP LENGTH	HEEL-TO-TOE LENGTH	TOE LENGTH
CHILDREN				
3–4	5¼"	1"	3¼"	1"
5–6	5½"	1¼"	3¾"	1¼"
7–8	5¾"	1½"	4½"	1¼"
9–10	6¼"	1½"	5"	1½"
11–12	6¾"	1¾"	6"	1½"
13	7"	1¾"	6½"	1½"
1–2	7¼"	1¾"	6½"	1½"
3–4	7½"	2"	6¾"	1½"
WOMEN				
5	7¾"	2"	6¾"	1½"
6	7¾"	2¼"	7"	1¾"
7–8	8"	2¼"	7"	1¾"
9	8¼"	2¼"	7¼"	2"
10	8¼"	2½"	7½"	2"
11	8½"	2½"	7¾"	2"
MEN				
8–9	8¼"	2¼"	7¾"	2"
10	8½"	2½"	8"	2¼"
11	8½"	2½"	8¼"	2¼"
12	8½"	2¾"	8½"	2½"
13	8¾"	2¾"	8½"	2½"
14	8¾"	2¾"	8¾"	2½"
15	9"	2¾"	8¾"	2½"

KNITTING BASICS

The following techniques are for the socks in this book.

LONG-TAIL CAST ON

I prefer the long-tail cast on because its elasticity is great for the cuffs of socks. Of course, you can use any other method to cast on your socks. Use the one you are familiar with; it's less confusing and will work just fine.

1. Pull the tail end from the ball of yarn and let a sufficient amount hang down to accommodate the stitches to be cast on. Make a slipknot and slide it onto one of the needles. The tail end should face you. Hold the needle in your right hand.

Squeeze your left thumb and index finger together and spread the remaining three fingers straight out. Slip the thumb and index finger (still squeezed together) between the two strands of yarn so that the tail hangs over the thumb and the working yarn hangs over the index finger. Grab the two strands of yarn, which are lying across your palm, with the remaining three fingers and open the thumb and index finger to look like an imaginary gun. Make sure the inside of the left hand faces you and the needle tip points toward the thumb.

2. Move the needle toward you and all the way down until it reaches the base of the thumb. Slide the needle under the outside strand of yarn wrapped around the thumb and up through the loop in front of the thumb.

3. Now move the needle over and behind the strand of yarn wrapped around the index finger and scoop it up. Then guide the needle from the top back into the loop in front of the thumb, down and toward you. Let the thumb slip from under the yarn strand and gently pull the front strand down to tighten the stitch on the needle. Remember, you don't want the stitches too tight around the needle. Instead, they should be slightly loose with space left for you to start knitting the first round.

Repeat steps 2 and 3 until the required number of stitches have been cast on.

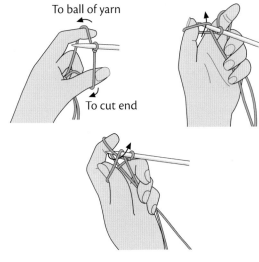

To ball of yarn

To cut end

DECREASES

There are several different ways to work decreases. In socks, decreases at the sides of the toe have to slant inward to accommodate the shape of the toes. This is crucial for both fit and appearance. The decreases need to slant to the right on the left side of the toe and slant to the left on the right side of the toe.

Right-Slanting Decrease

One right-slanting decrease is used in this book.

Knit two together (K2tog). Insert the needle into the next two stitches knitwise and knit them together as if they were one stitch. You've decreased one stitch.

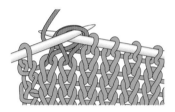

Left-Slanting Decreases

Two left-slanting decreases are used in this book.

Slip, slip, knit (ssk). Slip one stitch as if to knit; then slip the next stitch as if to knit. Insert the left-hand needle through the front of both stitches, but don't slip them back.

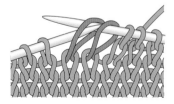

The right-hand needle is now sitting behind the left-hand needle. Use the right-hand needle to knit the two stitches together through the back loops. You've decreased one stitch.

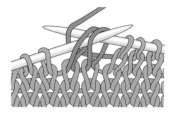

Slip, slip, purl (ssp). Slip, slip, purl is worked on the wrong side of your project, but it creates a left slant on the right side. To purl two stitches together through the back, both needle tips have to face in the same direction: to the right. Slip one stitch as if to knit; then slip the next stitch as if to knit. Now move both stitches back to the left-hand needle.

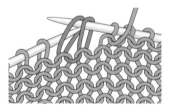

Insert the right-hand needle through the back loops of the slipped stitches from left to right, and then toward you to the front and left again. Now purl the two stitches off the left-hand needle. You've decreased one stitch.

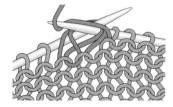

Central Decreases

These decreases slant neither left nor right and decrease two stitches. They are used in the Falling Leaves stitch pattern on page 77.

Double central decrease (sk2p). Slip one stitch as if to knit; knit the next two stitches together. Pass the slipped stitch over the knit stitch and off the right-hand needle. You've decreased two stitches.

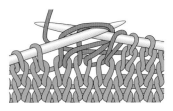

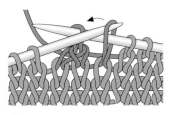

Slip two, knit one, pass two slipped stitches over (sl 2-K1-p2sso). Slip two stitches together as if to knit; knit one stitch. Pass the two slipped stitches over the knit stitch and off the right-hand needle. You've decreased two stitches.

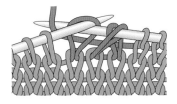

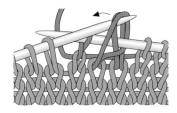

INCREASES

This book uses two variations of the "make one" stitch (M1). If the pattern doesn't indicate which one to work, use the one you are most comfortable with.

Make one stitch right (M1R). Slip the left-hand needle under the horizontal bar located between two stitches, from back to front. Notice how this "new" stitch is twisted. With the right-hand needle, knit into the front as with any other stitch. You've increased one stitch.

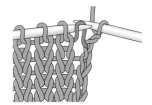

Insert left needle from back to front under horizontal bar.

Knit into front of stitch.

Make one stitch left (M1L). Slip the left-hand needle under the horizontal bar located between two stitches, from front to back. Notice how this "new" stitch is twisted. With the right-hand needle, knit through the back loop of this stitch. You've increased one stitch.

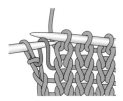

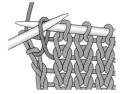

Insert left needle from front to back through "running thread."

Knit into back of stitch.

SHORT-ROW HEELS

Short rows are used to shape some of the heels in this book. Instead of working all the way across a row, you knit part way, turn, and work back. One way to do this is called "wrap and turn" (w&t) and is done differently depending on whether you're working a knit row or a purl row. Work to the point where you want to turn, and then work as follows.

Wrap and turn on a knit row. Slip the next stitch as if to purl with the yarn in back; bring the yarn forward between the needles (except when working the first w&t; here, bring the yarn forward around the slipped stitch). Move the slipped stitch back to the left-hand needle and move the yarn to the back away from you, between the needles. Turn and work the next row.

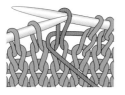 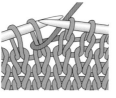

Slip stitch as if to purl. Move yarn to front of work and slip stitch back to left needle.

Move yarn to back of work. Turn.

Wrap and turn on a purl row. Slip the next stitch as if to purl with the yarn in front; move the yarn to the back of the work between the needles (except when working the first w&t, here, bring the yarn forward around the slipped stitch). Move the slipped stitch back to the left-hand needle and bring the yarn to the front toward you, between the needles. Turn and work the next row.

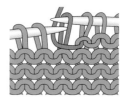 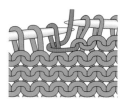

Slip stitch as if to purl. Move yarn to back of work and slip stitch back to left needle.

Move yarn toward you. Turn.

Once you've completed the wrap and turn as directed, you'll need to unwrap the stitches. This is also done differently depending on whether you're working on a knit row or purl row.

Unwrapping on a knit row. Knit to the first wrapped stitch; with the yarn in back and right-hand needle, pick up the wrap from the bottom up and leave it on the right-hand needle; then knit the stitch that was wrapped and pass the wrap over the stitch and off the needle.

Unwrapping on a purl row. Purl to the first wrapped stitch; with the yarn in front and right-hand needle, pick up the wrap on the right side (facing away from you) from the bottom up. Leave the wrap sitting on the right-hand needle; then purl the stitch that was wrapped and pass the wrap over the stitch and off the needle.

SEWN BIND OFF

This bind off creates a new stitch by weaving the yarn in and out of the knitted edge stitches. Do not pull the yarn tight as you might with a regular bind off.

Cut the working yarn four times the circumference of the cuff (approximately 35") and thread it onto a tapestry needle. Hold the work in your left hand and the needle in your right.

1. *Insert the needle into the first two stitches from right to left (as if to purl); gently pull the yarn through the stitches.

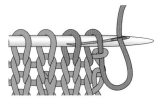

2. Reinsert the tapestry needle into the first stitch again, this time from left to right (as if to knit), and slip it off the needle. Gently pull the yarn through the stitch*. Repeat from * to * until one stitch is left; insert the right-hand needle as if to knit once more, slip the stitch off the left-hand needle, and ease it into the bound-off edge. When binding off two socks simultaneously, the last stitch of each set on the beginning needle needs to be slipped on a lockable marker and transferred to the beginning of the next needle in order to be worked.

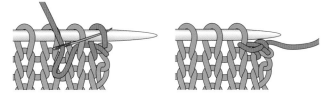

THE KITCHENER STITCH (GRAFTING)

Many knitters seem to be scared of the Kitchener stitch. While we may not quite understand it, its effect on a sock toe is simply amazing.

Hold the sock in your left hand, with right sides facing outward. The yarn tail hangs on the right side of the work and one needle sits in front of the other. Thread the yarn onto the tapestry needle. As you weave the yarn through the stitches, make sure you pass it under the needles, back and forth at all times.

When starting the Kitchener stitch in the traditional manner (work the first stitch on the front needle purlwise and work the first stitch on the back needle knitwise), I noticed a little ear in the corner. One day I started the process as described in step 1 and saw that there was no little ear. So you can choose whether to start in the traditional way or try my way.

1. To begin, weave the yarn through the first stitch on the front needle knitwise and push the stitch off the needle. Then weave the yarn through the next stitch on the front needle purlwise (now the first stitch) and leave it on the needle. Gently pull the yarn to match the tension of the rest of the knitted fabric. Weave the yarn through the first stitch on the back needle purlwise and push the stitch off the needle. Again, pull the yarn gently to create a new stitch as the toe closes up. Then weave the yarn through the next stitch on the back needle knitwise (now the first stitch) and leave it on the needle.

2. Weave the yarn through the first stitch on the front needle knitwise and push that stitch off the needle. Weave the yarn through the next stitch (now the first stitch) on the front needle purlwise and leave it on needle.

3. Weave the yarn through the first stitch on the back needle purlwise and push the stitch off the needle. Weave the yarn through the next stitch (now the first stitch) on the back needle knitwise and leave it on the needle.

Repeat steps 2 and 3 until there are two stitches left, one in front and one in back. Weave the yarn through the first stitch on the front needle knitwise, and then push that stitch off the needle. Weave the yarn through the first stitch on the back needle purlwise and push it off the needle. Pull the tapestry needle and yarn through the sock to the inside and weave in the tail.

Here's the short version.

Begin with:
    Front knit off, purl on
    Back purl off, knit on

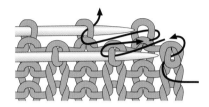

Continue with:
    Front knit off, purl on
    Back purl off, knit on

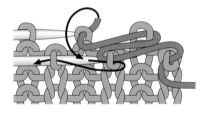

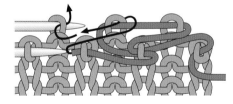

End with:
    Front knit off
    Back purl off

Sock Basics

The following tricks will not only assist in answering questions that go beyond common knitting techniques, they'll also help you easily create pair after pair of beautifully hand-knit socks.

AVOIDING TANGLING BALLS OF YARN ON THE HEEL FLAP

To avoid tangling your balls of yarn or accidentally adding stitches, try this: on the right side of the heel flap (16" needle), knit stitches of sock 1 and let the working yarn hang behind and over the cable of the 24" needle. Before beginning the wrong-side row, make sure that the working yarn hanging in the middle now lies over and behind the cable of the 16" needle.

On the wrong side of the heel flap, purl the stitches of sock 1 and let the working yarn hang down toward you, over the cable of the 24" needle. Before beginning the right-side row, make sure the working yarn in the middle remains over the cable of the 24" needle but now hangs away from you.

CLOSING THE GUSSET GAP

In her book *Sensational Knitted Socks* (Martingale & Company, 2005), Charlene Schurch shows a wonderful way to avoid the hated gap or hole that often occurs when picking up stitches for the gusset. This seems to plague gussets and sock knitters all over the world. I've modified this step a little to suit my knitting needs and it works perfectly.

Look closely at the gusset corner and find the last horizontal bar that connects an instep stitch with a heel-flap stitch. To close the gap, pick up both stitches by inserting your knitting needle into the heel-flap stitch

from front to back, and then into the instep stitch from back to front. You now have both stitches sitting on your right-hand needle. Knit them together, creating the extra corner stitch. Follow these directions for picking up one stitch wherever you see "PU 1 gusset st."

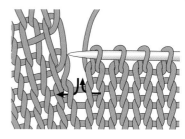

Picking up stitches
when both were knit

GAUGE AND GUSSET STITCHES

Tension is a knitter's thumbprint, belonging only to that person. We may get the correct stitch count per inch for width by manipulating the needle size, but at the same time, we can still have a different row count than suggested in a pattern.

Throughout the book you'll find expressions such as "about 2½"" or "approx 7"" rather than "work X number of rows." Everybody can reach 2" but not everybody can reach it with the number of rows expected for the pattern. Remember, the amount of gusset stitches instructed to be picked up is merely a guideline and you may end up with a few stitches more or less. Take a look at your heel-flap edge; each slipped stitch equals two worked rows, and the rule of thumb is to pick up one gusset stitch per two rows. You'll easily follow this guideline by simply picking up one stitch in each slipped stitch for your gusset. Just remember to pick up the same number for each side. The gusset decrease doesn't depend on a certain number of stitches; rather you'll repeat it until the original stitch count has been reached once more.

HEEL-FLAP EDGES

There is an easy way to get beautiful heel-flap edges with clearly visible stitches that make it easy to pick up stitches when creating the gusset. Unless otherwise instructed, always slip the first stitch purlwise with the yarn in front and knit the last stitch of every row.

ITALICIZED INSTRUCTIONS IN HEEL TURNS

You'll notice that there are some italicized instructions in the heel turn. The italics indicate a change of some sort. For example, the first stitch of row 1 (right side) has to be slipped purlwise with the yarn in front to stay true to the side of the heel flap. Once you begin to turn the heel and are working within a row, the first stitch of a right-side row has to be slipped knitwise with the yarn in back.

Example:

Row 1 (RS): Sl 1 wyif, K10 (12, 12), K2tog, K1, turn.
Row 2 (WS): Sl 1 wyif, P3 (5, 3), ssp, P1, turn.
Row 3: Sl 1 *kw wyib*, K4 (6, 4), K2tog, K1, turn.

A similar rule applies to the last stitch on the wrong-side rows. As long as you're working within a row, the last stitch gets purled, but when you get to the last wrong-side row, you'll have to knit the last stitch to accommodate the end stitch of the heel flap.

KNOTS AND TAILS

When working on your socks, you may encounter an irregularity or even a knot in your yarn. This seems to hold true especially for hand-dyed yarns.

I highly recommend that you cut and restart the yarn past the problem, leaving tails on both the end and the beginning of the new strand. These tails will be woven in later. If you decide to continue and knit the faulty yarn, it could very well open and unravel later. Once this happens, there are no tails to fix the weak spot and all your hard work will go into the trash.

To weave in the tails, slip the tapestry needle through the yarn strands, actually splitting them (rather than the traditional way of going under and over the yarn strands) in a wavelike manner. This makes the tail invisible from the right side of the fabric. You can weave in horizontally, vertically, or diagonally—whichever you prefer.

PERFECT GUSSET TRIANGLE

This is an optional technique. If you've ever knit socks from the cuff down, you'll know how the decrease turns the gusset into a perfect triangle. Well, that's what I expected to see as I decreased the gusset stitches of my toe-up socks, but it didn't happen. Instead the decrease finished early and left a flat edge rather than a beautiful point. I didn't like that at all. If you're as obsessive about wanting a perfect triangle as I am, decrease once more as indicated in the pattern instructions for your socks.

REINFORCING YOUR SOCKS

Some people like to reinforce the heels of their socks. There are two ways to do this—by carrying along a reinforcement yarn or by using smaller needles. Some yarn manufacturers include a spool of reinforcement yarn inside their skein of sock yarn. Or you can buy cards of reinforcement yarn at your local yarn shop. On cuff-down socks, add the reinforcement yarn when you start the heel flap and carry it through the heel turn. On toe-up socks, add the yarn at the heel turn and carry it up through the "mock" heel flap.

Using smaller needles will make the knitted fabric denser. Simply change to a smaller needle size before beginning to work the heel flap or heel turn. Then change back to the regular needle for the remainder of the sock.

SLIPPING STITCHES

When I teach my sock workshops, a lot of students ask me which way to slip the stitches from one needle to the other. When you read a pattern and it instructs you to slip one or more stitches without specifying whether to do so as if to knit or as if to purl, you are expected to slip your stitches as if to purl. Unless your pattern tells you specifically to slip the stitches knitwise, you'll *always* slip them purlwise.

TIGHTENING STITCHES AT THE BEGINNING OF A ROUND

In order to tighten the working yarn at the beginning of each set of stitches, try this: knit the first two stitches in pattern, and then pause to pull the strand really tight before continuing the row. After knitting the first few rows, it may seem that no matter how tight you pull your yarn, a slight gap remains at each turn. It will disappear completely as long as you remember to continue to knit the first two stitches, and then pull the strand tightly every time. Should the closing of the round remain uneven, you can always ease it into shape as you weave in your tail at the end.

UNDERSTANDING ROWS AND ROUNDS

For many of my students, the hardest question to answer when knitting two socks on circular needles is: is it a row or is it a round? Well, it's both. Look at your work. There are two separate projects on your needles for the basic pattern: sock one with 40 (44, 48) stitches and sock two with 40 (44, 48) stitches. Each sock is divided into two halves; one half with 20 (22, 24) stitches sits on the 24" needle and the other half with 20 (22, 24) stitches sits on the 16" needle. When you begin to knit, you'll work two halves on one needle, which is a row. When you get to the end of sock two on one needle, you turn your work (this is one half of the round) and knit the other two halves of your socks once again in a row. Then you'll turn your work again, thus completing two rows, which equal one complete round.

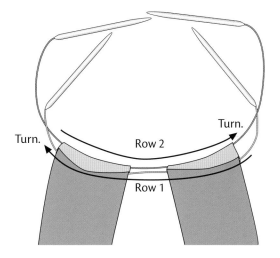

Unless otherwise specified, the pattern will list rounds only, and each round consists of two rows (16" and 24" needles). For example, if the instructions given for round one are:

Rnd 1: K1, M1R, knit to last st, M1L, K1. Rep for sock 2. (20 sts per sock)

Then it means that you work the rows as follows.

Row 1 on 16" needle: K1, M1R, knit to last st, M1L, K1. Rep for sock 2. (20 sts per sock)

Row 2 on 24" needle: K1, M1R, knit to last st, M1L, K1. Rep for sock 2. (20 sts per sock)

For every round, you'll work the same instructions on the 16" needle and the 24" needle.

CUFF-DOWN SOCKS

Over the past several years, I've taught many knitters how to knit two socks at a time on two circular needles. At first, this technique can be challenging and your brain may rebel and take a while to adjust to the various steps necessary. But knit on patiently, and after 2" to 3" your persistence will be rewarded! The chore of learning this method will quickly turn into a liberating thrill ride as you watch your pair of socks grow faster and faster until suddenly they're done and ready to be worn. I hope you'll enjoy making two at a time as much as many sock knitters do. For us, the "second sock syndrome" has finally become obsolete.

PAGE 19

PAGE 29

PAGE 34

PAGE 39

Women's Basic Cuff-Down Socks

For your first pair of two socks on two needles, consider choosing a light-colored worsted-weight yarn, which will make it easier for you to see and keep track of the stitches on your needles. I used Cascade 220 Tweed in light gray. I love the way this yarn works up as well as the way it wears. However, these socks will need to be hand washed because 100% wool will felt, shrink, and lose its elasticity if machine washed—something to consider when picking your yarn.

Skill level: Easy ◼◼☐☐

Sizes: Women's Small (Medium, Large)

To fit shoe sizes: 5–7 (8–9½, 10–12)

MATERIALS

1 skein of 220 Tweed from Cascade (90% Peruvian highland wool, 10% Donegal tweed; 100 g/3.5 oz; 200 m/220 yds) in color 7616 (wind 2 even-sized balls from the skein so you have 1 ball for each sock) **(4)**

2 size 5 (3.75 mm) circular needles (16" and 24")

Point protectors

2 stitch markers

Tapestry needle

GAUGE

6 sts = 1" in St st

Cure for a Tight Cast On

If you hate your chronically tight cast on as much as I do, try this: hold one end of both circular needles together and cast on over both needles. When you have the required number of stitches, simply pull out the 16" needle and voilà! You now have an easy-access cast on and won't have to fight itty-bitty stitches in your first row.

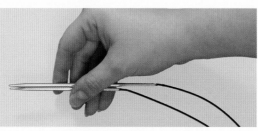

Needles held together as one

Stitches cast on using two needles

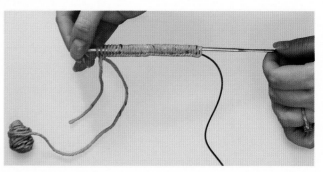

Stitches on the 24" needle after pulling out the 16" needle

SETTING UP YOUR CIRCULAR NEEDLES

CO 40 (44, 48) sts for your first sock using 1 of your 2 balls of yarn and 24" needle. Your work should look like figure 1.

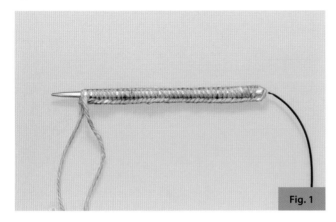

Fig. 1

Sl 20 (22, 24) sts pw from 24" needle onto 16" needle. The working strand of yarn (the one attached to your ball) as well as the open end of your sock should now face away from needle tips and toward cables (fig. 2).

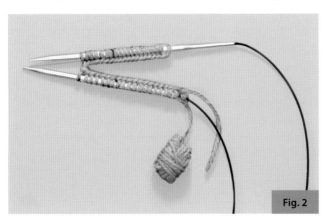

Fig. 2

Push all sts simultaneously to other end of both needles. The working yarn should now hang from tip of your 16" needle and the open side of your sock should face needle ends (fig. 3).

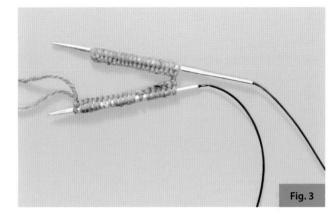

Fig. 3

To close rnd for first sock, first make sure sts aren't twisted and CO edge faces neatly inward. Thread tail onto a tapestry needle and weave it through first st on opposite side (fig. 4). Using tail and working yarn, tie a tight double knot to close rnd of sock 1.

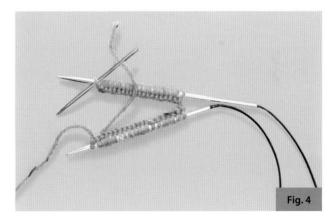

Fig. 4

For sock 2, use second ball of yarn and ignore sock 1. Slide sts from sock 1 closer to cables or put point protectors on tips. Using either the 24" needle or the 2-needle cast-on method, CO 40 (44, 48) sts on empty end(s) of your circular needles. Your work should look like figure 5.

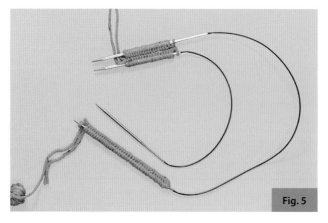

Fig. 5

Use empty 16" needle tip and sl 20 (22, 24) sts pw onto it. The working yarn as well as the open end of sock 2 should both face away from needle tips and toward cables (fig. 6).

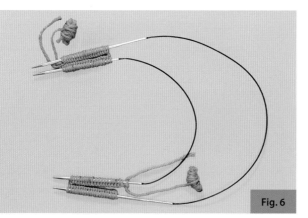

Fig. 6

As before, sl tail onto tapestry needle and, after making sure your sts are not twisted and CO edge is facing inward, thread it through first st of opposite side. Using working yarn and tail, tie a tight double knot to close gap. Scoot sock 2 along cables toward sock 1. Your needles and project should look like figure 7.

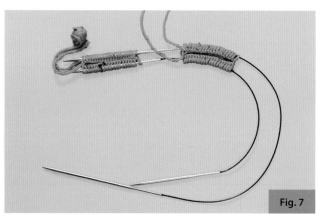

Fig. 7

You're now ready to knit the first row and round.

Let's knit the first row (half a rnd) step by step. Before you beg, notice that needles are parallel and ends face away from each other. We'll call this arrangement "row start position." Place point protector on each end of 24" needle because you'll be knitting sts on 16" needle first. Scoot sock 1 of row 1 close to needle tips and let sock 2 "rest" on cables. Holding needles in your left hand with working yarn at tips, make sure 24" needle sits slightly behind 16" one. Working yarn hangs between both needles for sock 1. Strand of yarn for sock 2 should lie over and behind cable of 24" needle. This way it will already be set up for later use without getting tangled or accidentally creating an extra st.

Pull end of 24" needle right and down so that sts sitting on it slide onto its cable. With your right hand, PU empty end of 16" needle and get ready to knit your first row. Make sure you squeeze tip of your 16" needle and cable of 24" needle tight tog; this will prevent gap from forming (fig. 8).

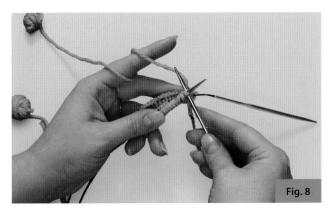

Fig. 8

CUFFS

Beg with 20 (22, 24) sts of sock 1: K1, pm, *P1, K1, rep from * to last st, P1.

The st marker you've just placed indicates beg of rnd from now on. Notice how needle position has changed after you've finished ribbing first 20 (22, 24) sts. The 16" needle is no longer in its row start position; tips are now facing each other. This is an excellent reminder that you have not completed the row and that you still have to work 20 (22, 24) sts of cuff for sock 2. Your work should look like figure 9.

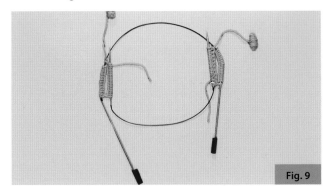

Fig. 9

Slide sts of sock 1 away from needle tip and let it rest. Make sure working yarn hangs behind 16" needle as well as over and behind cable of 24" needle. Scoot cuff sts of second sock close to tip of needle, making sure working yarn is picked up straight from 24" needle and doesn't create an extra st.

Again, squeeze needle tip and cable together to avoid creating a gap. Once more, you'll work K1, P1 ribbing for cuff.

You've just completed 1 row or first half of a rnd for your socks. Notice how needles have opened up and lie parallel once again. Looking at your work, you'll see that half of each cuff has been worked (fig. 10).

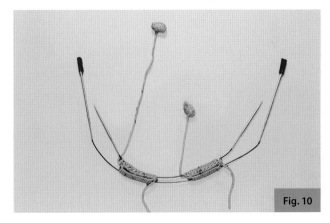

Fig. 10

To start second row of first rnd, turn your work so that unribbed sts face you and needle tips with working yarn attached are in your left hand. This time you'll knit off the 24" needle, so switch point protectors to tips of 16" needle. *Sock 2 on 16" needle now becomes sock 1 on 24" needle.* Remember to switch balls as you switch socks and make sure that working strand of yarn hangs between the two needles and resting strand of yarn lies over and behind back cable.

Align tips and hold the 16" needle *slightly behind* 24" one. As before, pull back needle (16") right and forward so its sts sl onto cable. Squeeze needle tip (24") and cable (16") close tog and start ribbing.

Notice how tips of 24" needle face each other after you've worked cuff for sock 1. Remember that you're only done with half of this row. You still have to knit cuff for sock 2 to finish row completely. Once needles are parallel again, you should be ready to start first row of next rnd at st marker.

You've finished a complete round for your socks and your needles are once again in row start position (fig. 11).

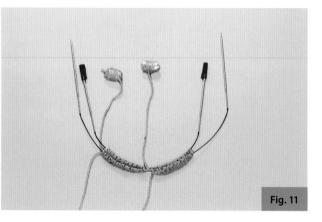

Fig. 11

Depending on your preference, cont to work cuff in ribbing for 1½" to 2" using previous guidelines. The repetitions will help you quickly get the hang of this technique. Remember to switch your point protectors onto tips of resting needle. This will help you remember and get used to using correct needle to knit with. Soon you'll feel confident enough and won't need them anymore (fig. 12).

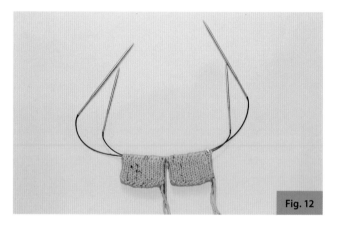

Fig. 12

LEGS

After the cuffs have reached desired length, beg St st on leg (knit every rnd). Here again, you decide length; how long do you want your sock leg to be (fig. 13)?

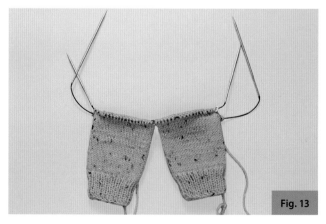

Fig. 13

The legs are done.

HEEL FLAPS

The heel flap is worked back and forth in rows on 20 (22, 24) sts on 16" needle, which also carries st marker. To create flap, knit in St st (knit 1 row, purl 1 row) across both socks. Before you beg, remove st marker and cover tips of 24" needle with point protectors.

For heel flap, always sl first st of each set and knit last one. This will make it easier to see edge sts later on when you have to pick them up.

Unless otherwise specified, sl all sts pw.

Row 1 (RS): Sl 1 wyif, *K1, sl 1 wyib, rep from * to last st, K1. Rep for sock 2.

Row 2 (WS): Sl 1 wyif, purl to last st, K1. Rep for sock 2.

Work rows 1 and 2 another 10 times for total of 22 rows (approx 2¼" to 2½"), ending with completed purl row. Heel flaps should measure approx 2¼" to 2½" (figs. 14 and 15).

The finished heel flap, wrong (purl) side

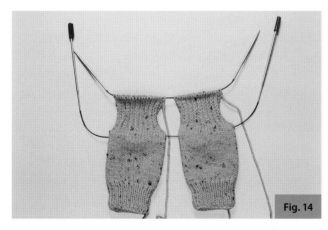

The finished heel flap, right (knit) side

HEEL TURNS

The heel is turned with short rows, which means that you are going to work back and forth within a row rather than completing it. This technique will leave unworked sts on your needle, and both heels cannot be worked at same time. Therefore, each heel has to be worked separately as follows. For explanation of italicized instructions in heel turn, see page 16.

Sock 1

All Sizes

Row 1 (RS): Sl 1 wyif, K10 (12, 12), K2tog, K1, turn.

Row 2 (WS): Sl 1 wyif, P3 (5, 3), ssp, P1, turn.

Row 3: Sl 1 *kw wyib*, K4 (6, 4), K2tog, K1, turn.

Row 4: Sl 1 wyif, P5 (7, 5), ssp, P1, turn.

Row 5: Sl 1 kw wyib, K6 (8, 6), K2tog, K1, turn.

Row 6: Sl 1 wyif, P7 (9, 7), ssp, P1, turn.

Row 7: Sl 1 kw wyib, K8 (10, 8), K2tog, K1, turn.

Small and Medium

Row 8: Sl 1 wyif, P9 (11), ssp, K1, turn.

Row 9: Sl 1 *wyif,* knit to end of row. *Do not turn your work.* [12 (14) sts rem]

Large

Row 8: Sl 1 wyif, P9, ssp, P1, turn.

Row 9: Sl 1 kw wyib, K10, K2tog, K1, turn.

Row 10: Sl 1 wyif, P11, ssp, *K1,* turn.

Row 11: *Sl 1 pw wyif,* knit to end of row. *Do not turn your work.* (14 sts rem)

First heel is turned. You should have 12 (14, 14) sts left on your needle. Cont with same needle tip, PU 11 (13, 13) sts along left side of heel flap. Then PU 1 st (the 12th, 14th, 14th) st in corner of your gusset. See "Closing the Gusset Gap" on page 15.

After you've picked up and knitted total of 12 (14, 14) gusset sts, this sock gets to rest while you work on turning heel of sock 2 (fig. 16).

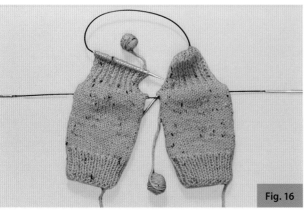

One heel has been turned and 12 (14, 14) gusset sts have been picked up.

Sock 2

Before you beg second heel, notice that tips of your 16" needle are facing each other; row is only half complete. Move sock 1 off RH needle and onto cable. PU needle that holds second heel in your left hand and turn heel of sock 2 as for sock 1.

After you've turned second heel, you should have 12 (14, 14) sts left on your needle. Cont with same needle tip you just worked with, PU 11 (13, 13) sts along side of heel flap, then PU 1 gusset st in corner as before (fig. 17).

Both heels have been turned and two sets of gusset sts have been picked up.

Turn your work so that the instep sts are facing you, with 20 (22, 24) sts per sock. Switch point protectors to 16" needle and knit even across instep sts for both socks using the 24" needle. Remember to push sts of sock 1 back onto cable so you'll be able to tighten working yarn after second st. Turn.

Heel sts are facing you once again. Switch point protectors to 24" needle. PU and knit gusset sts on second side of sock 1, this time starting at gusset corner and working up heel flap. With your left hand, PU heel flap of sock you're getting ready to work on. With your right hand, PU opposite end of 16" needle and guide it across front of work to heel flap you're holding. Working yarn should be ready and waiting in corner of gusset of this sock. Remember, this time you're starting in gusset corner and working your way up heel flap.

PU 1 gusset st in corner as before. Pull working yarn tight and cont to PU 11 (13, 13) more sts along side of heel flap. After all sts have been picked up, you should be at heel. Knit across first 6 (7, 7) heel sts and pm. Cont to knit across rem heel sts as well as previously picked-up gusset sts on other side. After you're done with sock 1, push it away from tip and onto cable of 16" needle.

Using second ball and needle you're currently holding in your right hand, PU 1 gusset st in corner of sock 2. Pull working yarn nice and tight and cont to PU 11 (13, 13) more sts along the side of heel flap. Knit across first 6 (7, 7) heel sts and pm. Cont to knit across rem heel sts as well as previously picked-up gusset sts on other side. The 2 st markers will help you check your work and dec evenly in next step (fig. 18).

Fig. 18

Both heels have been turned and all gusset sts have been picked up.

Both heels are turned and all gusset sts have been picked up. From now on, you'll once again knit in rows as well as rnds. If you still need a little help remembering, cont to switch point protectors to tips of resting needle.

The 24" needle is holding instep sts with 20 (22, 24) sts per sock. The 16" needle is holding sole and gusset sts with 36 (42, 42) sts per sock; total of 56 (64, 66) sts per sock.

GUSSET DECREASES

Turn your work so instep sts are facing you and knit across them. Turn work so sole sts are facing you. From now on, you'll knit even across instep sts (24" needle) and dec gusset sts on 16" needle only.

Sl markers as you get to them.

Rnd 1

Row 1 (sole): Knit across sock 1 to last 3 sts, K2tog, K1. Rep for sock 2.

Row 2 (instep): Knit even across instep sts of both socks.

Rnd 2

Row 1 (sole): K1, ssk, knit to end of sock 1. Rep for sock 2.

Row 2 (instep): Knit even across instep sts of both socks.

Rep rnds 1 and 2 until original number of sts, total of 40 (44, 48) sts per sock rem, with 20 (22, 24) sts per half. Remove 1 st marker and leave 1 to mark needle that starts rnd.

FEET

Work foot in St st (knit each rnd) until it measures approx 7½ (8, 8½)" from back of heel, or until it reaches base of your big toe when sock is tried on (fig. 19).

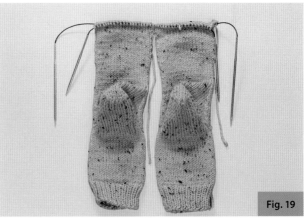

Fig. 19

Work until foot reaches 7½ (8, 8½)" or base of big toe.

TOES

Shaped toe is done by dec on both sides of foot, 2 sts on sole side and 2 sts on instep side, for total of 4 sts on EOR. You should be ready to beg dec on sole side (16" needle).

Rnd 1

Rows 1 (sole) and 2 (instep): K1, ssk, knit to last 3 sts of sock 1, K2tog, K1. Rep for sock 2.

Rnd 2: Knit even across both needles.

Rep rnds 1 and 2 until total of 20 sts rem per sock (10 sts per half), ending with rnd 2.

Rep rnd 1 until total of 12 sts rem per sock (6 sts per half).

Cut yarn for both socks, leaving generous tail about 7" to 10".

To close toe, work with both needles (instep and sole sts) at same time for each sock. Push all sts for sock 1 close to ends of both needles and hold them in your left hand. As before, one needle will sit behind the other, and front one should sit slightly lower than back one. Working yarn should be attached to needle held in back (in this case, 24" needle). Weave toe sts tog with Kitchener st on page 13.

Weave in all ends and immediately try your socks on. Congratulations! You've just finished your first pair of socks on two circular needles. Following are more awesome cuff-down patterns to make.

Bobbles and Slips

Hand-painted variegated yarns are gorgeous! I, for one, work these little gems up greedily because I want to see what designs and hues will splash across my sock next. But plain stockinette can become rather boring no matter how splendid the fibers, and many patterns, breathtaking in solid colors, simply disappear when worked with multicolored yarn. Enter the underrated slip stitch—simple in construction yet very effective when put into action with color. Enjoy!

Skill level: Intermediate ◼◼◼▢

Sizes: Women's Small (Medium, Large)
To fit shoe sizes: 5–6 (7–9, 10–11)

MATERIALS

2 skeins of Paca Peds Superwash Alpaca Sock Yarn from the Alpaca Yarn Company (65% superwash wool, 20% superfine alpaca, 15% nylon; approx 3.5 oz/100g; 360 yds) in color 606 **❶**

Small: 2 size 2 (2.75 mm) circular needles (16" and 24")

Medium and Large: 2 size 3 (3.25 mm) circular needles (16" and 24")

Cable needle

Point protectors

2 lockable stitch markers

2 stitch markers

Tapestry needle

GAUGE

Small: 7½ sts = 1" in St st on size 2 needles

Medium and Large: 7 sts = 1" in St st on size 3 needles

SPECIAL INSTRUCTIONS

C3L: Sl 1 st to cn and hold at front, K2, K1 from cn.

C3R: Sl 2 sts to cn and hold at back, K1, K2 from cn.

Bobble: Work K1, K1 tbl, K1, K1 tbl, K1 in next st, turn, knit 3 rows (WS, RS, WS) across these 5 sts only, working last row a bit more loosely. On next RS row, K5tog tbl. It's easiest to use size 5 or 6 crochet hook to help you knit 5 sts tog, and then place new st on RH needle.

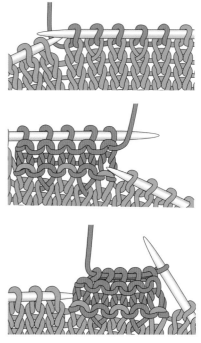

CUFFS

Using appropriate-size needle for your sock size, CO and set up 60 sts per sock (30 sts per half). The 16" needle marks beg of rnd.

Work 10 rnds in St st (knit each rnd). Work cuff in K1, P1 ribbing for another 8 rnds.

LEGS

Knit 1 rnd.

Beg bobble patt.

Rnd 1: *Bobble, K4, rep from * to end. Rep for sock 2.

Rnd 2

Notice that st right before bobble st is rather big and that there's a huge gap between the two sts. Quick fix in this rnd will take care of those nasty spaces perfectly!

Rows 1 and 2: *Knit to bobble, with LH needle, PU topmost horizontal bar between last worked st and bobble st from *back to front* (similar to a M1R), knit bar and bobble st tog to close gap, rep from * to end. Rep for sock 2.

Rnd 3: Knit even across both needles.

Rnd 4: K2, *bobble, K4, rep from * to last 3 sts, bobble, K2. Rep for sock 2.

Rnds 5 and 6: Rep rnd 3 twice.

Rnd 7: *Bobble, K4, rep from * to end. Rep for sock 2.

Rnd 8: Rep rnd 3.

Rnd 9: K6, (M1, K6) 4 times, rep for sock 2. (68 sts per sock)

Rnd 10: K12, (M1, K11) twice, rep for sock 2. (72 sts per sock)

Rnd 11: K8, (M1, K7) 4 times, rep for sock 2. (80 sts per sock)

Beg sl-st patt.

Unless otherwise specified, sl all sts pw.

Rnd 1: (Sl 1 wyib, K3) rep to end. Rep for sock 2.

Rnd 2: (Sl 1 wyib, K3) rep to end. Rep for sock 2.

Rnd 3: *C3L, K1, rep from * to end. Rep for sock 2.

Rnd 4: Knit across both needles.

Rnd 5: *Sl 1 wyib, K3 rep from * to end. Rep for sock 2.

Rnd 6: Sl first st on lockable st marker, K3, *sl 1, K3, rep from * to end. Rep for sock 2.

Rnd 7: (K1, C3R) rep to last 2 sts, sl last 2 sts on cn, move st from lockable st marker to LH needle and knit, K2 from cn as usual. Rep for sock 2.

Rnd 8

Row 1 (16"): Knit to last st, sl last st on lockable marker. Rep for sock 2. Turn.

Row 2 (24"): Sl st from st marker to LH needle tip and knit across all sts of sock 1. Sl last (knitted) st onto lockable st marker. Rep for sock 2.

Rnd 9

Row 1: Sl st from marker to RH needle wyib, K3, *sl 1 wyib, K3, rep from * to end. Rep for sock 2.

Row 2: (Sl 1 wyib, K3), rep to end. Rep for sock 2.

Rep rnds 2–9 until leg measures approx 7" from rolled cuff edge or until desired length, ending with rnd 4.

Dec Rnds

Rnd 1: K8, (K2tog, K6) 4 times, rep for sock 2. (72 sts per sock)

Rnd 2: K12, (K2tog, K10) twice, rep for sock 2. (68 sts per sock)

Rnd 3: K6, (K2tog, K5) 4 times, rep for sock 2. (60 sts per sock)

Rnds 4–6: Knit even across both needles.

HEEL FLAPS

The heel flap is worked back and forth in rows on 16" needle only. Place point protectors on resting needle before you beg.

Row 1 (RS): Sl 1 wyif, *K1, sl 1 wyib, rep from * to last st, K1. Rep for sock 2.

Row 2 (WS): Sl 1 wyif, purl to last st, K1. Rep for sock 2.

Rep rows 1 and 2 until heel flap measures approx 2 (2¼, 2½)".

HEEL TURNS

Heel is turned with short rows; therefore, each heel is worked separately. Beg with sock 1 on 16" needle. For explanation of italicized instructions in heel turn, see page 16.

Sock 1

Row 1 (RS): Sl 1 wyif, K16, K2tog, K1, turn.

Row 2 (WS): Sl 1 wyif, P5, ssp, P1, turn.

Row 3: Sl 1 *kw wyib*, K6, K2tog, K1, turn.

Row 4: Sl 1 wyif, P7, ssp, P1, turn.

Row 5: Sl 1 kw wyib, K8, K2tog, K1, turn.

Row 6: Sl 1 wyif, P9, ssp, P1, turn.

Row 7: Sl 1 kw wyib, K10, K2tog, K1, turn.

Row 8: Sl 1 wyif, P11, ssp, P1, turn.

Row 9: Sl 1 kw wyib, K12, K2tog, K1, turn.

Row 10: Sl 1 wyif, P13, ssp, P1, turn.

Row 11: Sl 1 kw wyib, K14, K2tog, K1, turn.

Row 12: Sl 1 wyif, P15, ssp, K1, turn.

Row 13: Sl 1 *pw wyif,* knit to end, *do not turn.* (18 sts rem)

Cont with same needle tip, PU 18 sts along heel flap, PU 1 gusset st in corner (see "Closing the Gusset Gap" on page 15) for total of 19 sts.

Sock 2

Move sock to cable and turn heel for sock 2 as for sock 1. After second heel is turned, cont with same needle tip, PU 18 sts along heel flap, PU 1 gusset st in corner for total of 19 sts. Turn. If necessary, switch point protectors to appropriate needle. Knit even across all instep sts. Turn.

Beg at gusset corner of sock 1, *PU 1 gusset st in corner, then PU 18 sts along second side of heel flap for total of 19 sts. K9 heel sts, pm, knit across rem heel and gusset sts on other side. Rep from * for sock 2, beg in gusset corner. Turn. Knit even across all instep sts. Turn.

Both heels have been turned and all gusset sts have been picked up. From now on, you'll once again knit in rows as well as rnds. If you need help remembering, cont to switch point protectors to tips of resting needle. There are 68 sts on 16" needle and 30 sts for all sizes on 24" needle.

GUSSET DECREASES

Only sole sts are dec.

Rnd 1

Row 1 (sole): Knit across to last 3 sts, K2tog, K1. Rep for sock 2.

Row 2 (instep): Knit even across both socks.

Rnd 2

Row 1: K1, ssk, knit to end. Rep for sock 2.

Row 2: Knit even across both socks.

Rep rnds 1 and 2 until 30 sole sts rem on 16" needle per sock, matching number of instep sts for total of 60 sts per sock.

FOOT

Remove both st markers and knit even across sole and instep sts until foot measures approx 7 (7½, 8¼)" from back of heel, or until it reaches base of your big toe when sock is tried on. End with sts on 24" needle.

TOES

Beg with sole sts on 16" needle.

Rnd 1

Rows 1 (sole) and 2 (instep): K1, ssk, knit to last 3 sts, K2tog, K1. Rep for sock 2.

Rnds 2–4: Knit even across both needles.

Rnd 5

Rows 1 and 2: K1, ssk, knit to last 3 sts, K2tog, K1. Rep for sock 2.

Rnds 6 and 7: Knit even across both needles.

Rnd 8

Rows 1 and 2: K1, ssk, knit to last 3 sts, K2tog, K1. Rep for sock 2.

Rnds 9 and 10: Knit even across both needles.

Rnd 11

Rows 1 and 2: K1, ssk, knit to last 3 sts, K2tog, K1. Rep for sock 2.

Rnd 12: Knit even across both needles.

Rnd 13

Rows 1 and 2: K1, ssk, knit to last 3 sts, K2tog, K1. Rep for sock 2.

Rnd 14: Knit even across both needles.

Rnd 15

Rows 1 and 2: K1, ssk, knit to last 3 sts, K2tog, K1. Rep for sock 2.

Rnd 16: Knit even across both needles.

Rep rnd 15 only until 16 total sts rem per sock.

Cut yarn for both socks, leaving 10" tails, and use Kitchener st to graft toe sts tog (see page 13).

In Slipping Color

Jubilee from Blue Ridge Yarns is another hand-dyed fiber that tantalizes a knitter's palate! The color combinations are beautiful, but the short color sequences can make many patterns look rather messy and disorganized, which is especially sad after you've spent hours and hours working with a complicated pattern. Of course, you could always use those good old stripes again . . . naahh! Instead, here's another fun and easy slip-stitch pattern to try with astonishing results that will bring the wildest color combinations to life.

Skill level: Intermediate ◖◗◗◗◗◗

Sizes: Women's Small (Medium, Large)

To fit shoe sizes: 5–6 (7–9, 10–11)

MATERIAL

2 skeins of Jubilee from Blue Ridge Yarns (100% superwash merino wool; approx 50 g; 200 yds) in color Virginia Creeper 🄯2🄯

2 size 2 (2.75 mm) circular needles (16" and 24")

Cable needle

Point protectors

2 stitch markers

2 lockable stitch markers

Tapestry needle

GAUGE

7½ sts= 1" in St st

SLIP-STITCH PATTERN

Kw3: K1 wrapping yarn 3 times around needle.

C3R: Sl 2 sts on cn and hold in back, K1 then K2 from cn.

C3L: Sl 1 st on cn and hold in front, K2 then K1 from cn.

Rnd 1: K2, (Kw3 twice, K4) 4 (5, 5) times, Kw3 twice, K2. Rep for sock 2.

Rnd 2: K2, [(sl 1 dropping 2 wraps) twice, K4] 4 (5, 5) times, (sl 1 dropping 2 wraps) twice, K2. Rep for sock 2.

Rnds 3–5: K2, (sl 2, K4) 4 (5, 5) times, sl 2, K2. Rep for sock 2.

Rnd 6: (C3R, C3L) 5 (6, 6) times. Rep for sock 2.

Rep rnds 1–6 for patt.

CUFFS

CO and set up 54 (66, 66) sts [27 (33, 33) sts per half]. Work in K1, P1 ribbing for 2" or desired length. Because the st counts are uneven for each half, for cuff ribbing only, you'll beg and end row 1 with K1 and beg and end row 2 with P1.

Beginning of Round Reminder

Use the 16" needle to mark the beginning of the round from now on rather than a stitch marker, which would hinder the smooth knitting of the slip-stitch patt. If you don't feel confident enough to do this without a reminder, attach a lockable stitch marker to the cast-on edge of the first sock to be worked.

Inc Rnd

Small: K6, (M1, K7) 3 times, rep for sock 2. (60 sts per sock)

Medium and Large: K9, (M1, K8) 3 times, rep for sock 2. (72 sts per sock)

LEGS

Beg sl-st patt and work rnds 1–6 until leg measures approx 8" from CO edge or until desired length, ending with a completed row 6.

Dec Rnd

Small

Row 1 (16"): K1 and sl that st onto lockable marker, K7, (K2tog, K8) twice, K2tog. Rep for sock 2.

Row 2 (24"): K8, (K2tog, K8) twice, K2tog, sl st from marker to LH needle and K1. Rep for sock 2. (54 sts per sock: 26 sts on 16" needle and 28 sts on 24" needle)

Medium and Large

Rows 1 and 2: K3, K2tog, K3 (K2tog, K4) 3 times, (K2tog, K3) twice. Rep for sock 2. (60 sts per sock)

HEEL FLAPS

The heel flap is worked back and forth in rows on 16" needle only. Place point protectors on resting needle before you beg.

Row 1 (RS): Sl 1 wyif, *K1, sl 1 wyib, rep from * to last st, K1. Rep for sock 2.

Row 2 (WS): Sl 1 wyif, purl to last st, K1. Rep for sock 2.

Rep rows 1 and 2 until heel flap measures approx 2 (2¼, 2½)".

HEEL TURNS

The heel is turned with short rows; therefore, each heel is worked separately, beg with sock 1. Cont to work in rows and with same needle as for heel flap. For explanation of italicized instructions in heel turn, see page 16.

Sock 1

All Sizes

Row 1 (RS): Sl 1 wyif, K14 (16, 16), K2tog, K1, turn.

Row 2 (WS): Sl 1 wyif, P5, ssp, P1, turn.

Row 3: Sl 1 *kw wyib*, K6, K2tog, K1, turn.

Row 4: Sl 1 wyif, P7, ssp, P1, turn.

Row 5: Sl 1 kw wyib, K8, K2tog, K1, turn.

Row 6: Sl 1 wyif, P9, ssp, P1, turn.

Row 7: Sl 1 kw wyib, K10, K2tog, K1, turn.

Row 8: Sl 1 wyif, P11, ssp, P1, turn.

Row 9: Sl 1 kw wyib, K12, K2tog, K1, turn.

Small

Row 10: Sl 1 wyif, P13, ssp, K1, turn.

Row 11: Sl 1 *pw wyif*, K15, *do not turn.* (16 sts rem)

Medium and Large

Row 10: Sl 1 wyif, P13, ssp, P1, turn.

Row 11: Sl 1 kw wyib, K14, K2tog, K1, turn.

Row 12: Sl 1 wyif, P15, ssp, K1, turn.

Row 13: Sl 1 *pw wyif*, K17, *do not turn.* (18 sts rem)

Cont with same needle tip, PU 16 (18, 20) sts along heel flap, PU 1 gusset st in corner (see "Closing the Gusset Gap" on page 15) for total of 17 (19, 21) sts.

Sock 2

Move sock 1 to cable and turn heel as for sock 1. After second heel is turned, cont with same needle tip, PU 16 (18, 20) sts along heel flap, PU 1 gusset st in corner for total of 17 (19, 21) sts. Turn. Switch point protectors to appropriate needle. Knit even across all instep sts. Turn.

Beg at gusset corner of sock 1, *PU 1 gusset st in corner, then PU 16 (18, 20) sts along second side of heel flap for total of 17 (19, 21) sts. K8 (9, 9) heel sts, pm, knit across rem heel and gusset sts on other side. Rep from * for sock 2, beg in gusset corner. Turn. Knit even across all instep sts. Turn.

Both heels have been turned and all gusset sts have been picked up. From now on, you'll once again knit in rows as well as rnds. If you still need a little help remembering, cont to switch point protectors to tips of resting needle. There are 50 (56, 60) sts on 16" needle and 28 (30, 30) sts on 24" needle.

GUSSET DECREASES

Only sole sts are dec.

All Sizes

Rnd 1

Row 1 (sole): Knit across to last 3 sts, K2tog, K1. Rep for sock 2.

Row 2 (instep): Knit even across both socks.

Rnd 2

Row 1: K1, ssk, knit to end. Rep for sock 2.

Row 2: Knit even across both socks.

Rep rnds 1 and 2 until 26 (30, 30) sole sts rem on 16" needle per sock, added to 28 (30, 30) instep sts for total of 54 (60, 60) sts per sock.

Small

Rnd 1

Row 1: Knit even across heel sts. Rep for sock 2.

Row 2: K1 and sl st on lockable marker, knit to end of sock. Rep for sock 2.

Rnd 2

Row 1: Knit across to end of sock 1, sl st from marker to LH needle and knit it. Rep for sock 2.

Row 2: Knit even across both socks.

FOOT

Remove st markers and knit even across sole and instep sts until foot measures approx 7 (7½, 8¼)" from back of heel, or until it reaches base of your big toe when sock is tried on. End with sts on 24" needle.

TOES

Beg with sole sts on 16" needle.

Rnd 1

Rows 1 (sole) and 2 (instep): K1, ssk, knit to last 3 sts, K2tog, K1. Rep for sock 2.

Rnds 2–4: Knit even across both needles.

Rnd 5

Rows 1 and 2: K1, ssk, knit to last 3 sts, K2tog, K1. Rep for sock 2.

Rnds 7 and 8: Knit even across both needles.

Rnd 8

Rows 1 and 2: K1, ssk, knit to last 3 sts, K2tog, K1. Rep for sock 2.

Rnds 9 and 10: Knit even across both needles.

Rnd 11

Rows 1 and 2: K1, ssk, knit to last 3 sts, K2tog, K1. Rep for sock 2.

Rnd 12: Knit even across both needles.

Rnd 13

Rows 1 and 2: K1, ssk, knit to last 3 sts, K2tog, K1. Rep for sock 2.

Rnd 14: Knit even across both needles.

Rnd 15

Rows 1 and 2: K1, ssk, knit to last 3 sts, K2tog, K1. Rep for sock 2.

Rnd 16: Knit even across both needles.

Rep rnd 15 only until 14 (16, 16) total sts rem per sock.

Cut yarn for both socks, leaving a 7" to 10" tail, and use Kitchener st to graft toe sts tog for each sock (see page 13).

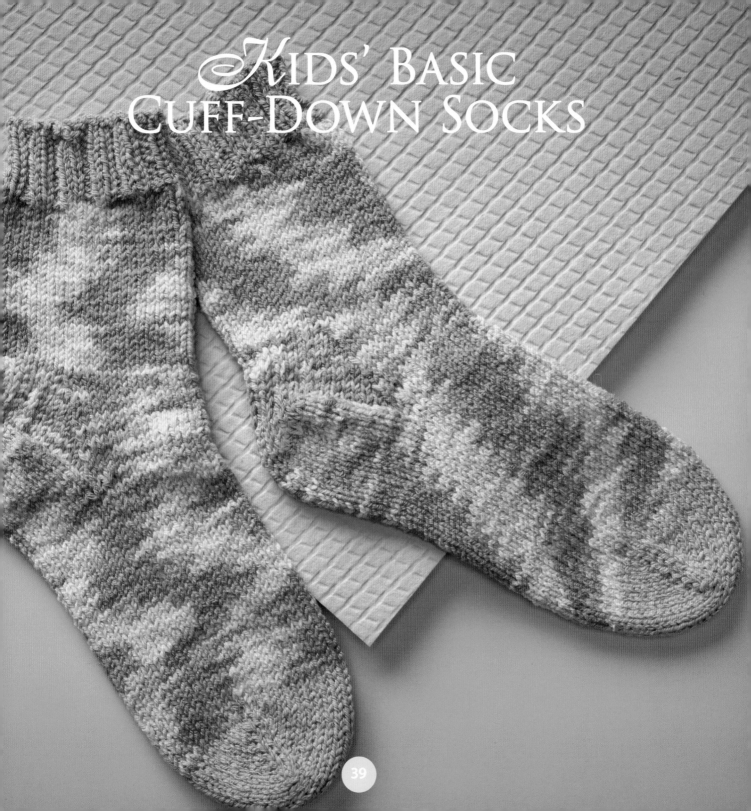

Kids' Basic Cuff-Down Socks

If you've ever gone in search of a sock pattern for kids ages 5–12, you've probably come to the realization that they're difficult to come by. You will find a ton of adorable baby-bootee patterns of course, and toddlers are still lucky with a few choices, but after that kids' sock patterns become rather limited. The size for the kids' socks in this book includes infants to 12-year-olds. The stitch numbers can serve as a base from which you can easily explore textured and colored patterns if you so choose.

You can choose to knit from the cuff down or from the toe up. The basic pattern for kids' cuff-down socks in fingering-weight yarn follows. The basic pattern for kids' toe-up socks using sport-weight yarn begins on page 78.

Skill level: Easy ◖■■□▷

Sizes: Infant (0–9 mos) [Extra Small (1–2 yrs), Small (3–5 yrs), Medium (6–8 yrs), Large (9–12 yrs)]

To fit shoe sizes: 1–3 (4–6, 7–10, 11–13, 1–4)

MATERIALS

MC 1 skein of Maizy from Crystal Palace Yarns (82% corn fiber, 18% elastic nylon; 50 g/1.75 oz; 204 yds/188.5 m) in color 1008 (①)

CC 1 skein of Maizy from Crystal Palace Yarns in color 1206

2 size 2 (2.75 mm) circular needles (16" and 24")

Point protectors

2 stitch markers

Tapestry needle

Note: You'll need 1 (1, 1, 1, 2) skein total if you make a solid-colored sock instead.

See "Striped Socks for Sport Fans" on page 42 to make a two-color striped sock.

GAUGE

8 sts = 1" in St st

Highlighting Your Size

Circle or highlight all numbers pertaining to the size socks you are making. That way you won't get confused and accidentally switch sizes while working on your project.

CUFFS

With CC, CO and set up 40 (44, 44, 48, 56) sts. [20 (22, 22, 24, 28) socks per half]

For cuff, work in K1, P1 or K2, P2 ribbing for approx 1 (1, 1, 1½, 1½)" or until preferred length.

LEGS

Switch to MC and work leg in St st (knit each rnd) until leg measures approx 1½ (2½, 3, 4, 5½)" from CO edge or until desired length.

HEEL FLAPS

The heel flap is worked in rows on 16" needle only. Place point protectors on resting needle before you beg.

Sl all sts pw unless otherwise specified.

Row 1 (RS): Sl 1 wyif, *K1, sl 1 wyib, rep from * to last st, K1.

Row 2 (WS): Sl 1 wyif, purl to last st, K1.

Rep rows 1 and 2 until heel flap measures 1 (1¼, 1½, 1¾, 1¾)", ending with completed purl row.

HEEL TURNS

Switch to CC.

The heel is turned with short rows; therefore, each heel is worked separately, beg with sock 1. Cont to work in rows and with same needle as for heel flap. For explanation of italicized instructions in heel turn, see page 16.

Sock 1

All Sizes

Row 1 (RS): Sl 1 wyif, K10 (12, 12, 12, 14) sts, K2tog, K1, turn.

Row 2 (WS): Sl 1 wyif, P3 (5, 5, 3, 3) sts, ssp, P1, turn.

Row 3: Sl 1 *kw wyib*, K4 (6, 6, 4, 4) sts, K2tog, K1, turn.

Row 4: Sl 1 wyif, P5 (7, 7, 5, 5) sts, ssp, P1, turn.

Row 5: Sl 1 kw wyib, K6 (8, 8, 6, 6) sts, K2tog, K1, turn.

Row 6: Sl 1 wyif, P7 (9, 9, 7, 7), ssp, P1, turn.

Row 7: Sl 1 kw wyib, K8 (10, 10, 8, 8) sts, K2tog, K1, turn.

Infant

Row 8: Sl 1 wyif, P9, ssp, K1.

Row 9: Sl 1 *pw wyif*, knit to end of row, *do not turn.* (12 sts)

Extra Small and Small

Row 8: Sl 1 wyif, P11 (11), ssp, K1, turn.

Row 9: Sl 1 *pw wyif*, knit to end of row, *do not turn.* (14 sts for both sizes)

Medium

Row 8: Sl 1 wyif, P9, ssp, P1, turn.

Row 9: Sl 1 kw wyib, K10, K2tog, K1, turn.

Row 10: Sl 1 wyif, P11, ssp, K1, turn.

Row 11: Sl 1 *pw wyif*, knit to end of row, *do not turn.* (14 sts)

Large

Row 8: Sl 1 wyif, P9, ssp, P1, turn.

Row 9: Sl 1 kw wyib, K10, K2tog, K1, turn.

Row 10: Sl 1 wyif, P11, ssp, K1, turn.

Row 11: Sl 1 kw wyib, K12, K2tog, K1, turn.

Row 12: Sl 1 wyif, P13, ssp, K1, turn.

Row 13: Sl 1 *pw wyif*, knit to end of row, *do not turn.* (16 sts)

For all sizes cont with same needle tip, PU 10 (12, 12, 14, 14) sts along side of heel flap, PU 1 gusset st in corner (see "Closing the Gusset Gap" on page 15) for total of 11 (13, 13, 15, 15) sts.

Sock 2

Move sock 1 to cable and turn heel for sock 2 as for sock 1. After second heel is turned, cont with same needle tip, PU 10 (12, 12, 14, 14) sts along left side of heel flap, PU 1 st in corner for total of 11 (13, 13, 15, 15) sts. Turn. Switch point protectors to appropriate needle.

Knit even across instep sts. Turn. Beg at gusset corner of sock 1, *PU 1 gusset st in corner, 10 (12, 12, 14, 14) sts along second side of heel flap for total of 11 (13, 13, 15, 15) sts, K6 (7, 7, 7, 8) heel sts, pm, knit across rem heel and gusset sts on other side. Rep from * for sock 2, beg at gusset corner. Turn. Knit even across all instep sts. Turn.

Both heels are turned and all gusset sts have been picked up. From now on, you'll once again knit in rows as well as rnds. Switch point protectors to tips of resting needle. There are 34 (40, 40, 44, 46) sts on 16" needle and 20 (22, 22, 24, 28) sts on 24" needle.

GUSSET DECREASES

Switch to MC.

Only sole sts are dec.

Rnd 1:

Row 1 (sole): Knit across to last 3 sts, K2tog, K1. Rep for sock 2.

Row 2 (instep): Knit even across all sts.

Rnd 2:

Row 1: K1, ssk, knit to end. Rep for sock 2.

Row 2: Knit even across all sts.

Rep rnds 1 and 2 until 20 (22, 22, 24, 28) sole sts rem on 16" needle per sock, matching number of instep sts for total of 40 (44, 44, 48, 56) sts per sock.

Remove both markers. The 16" needle marks beg of rnd.

FOOT

Knit even across sole and instep sts until foot measures approx 3½ (4, 4¾, 6¼, 7)" from back of heel.

TOES

Switch to CC.

Rnd 1:

Row 1 (sole) and row 2 (instep): K1, ssk, knit to last 3 sts, K2tog, K1. Rep for sock 2.

Rnd 2: Knit even across both needles.

Rep rnds 1 and 2 until total of 16 sts rem per sock (total of 32 sts on both needles), ending with rnd 2 and needle 2.

Rep rnd 1 once more, total of 12 sts rem per sock.

Cut yarn for both socks, leaving generous tail approx 10" long.

Use Kitchener sts to graft toe sts tog for each sock (page 13).

Striped Socks for Sports Fans

In Tennessee, we take our football seriously . . . our college football that is. During the season, everything is orange and white. The color grows on you and I had to knit a pair of orange-and-white striped baby socks, of course. What's your favorite team and what are its colors? Play a little and try your own ideas for striping!

For striped socks, purchase one skein each of your favorite team colors. To make stripes as I did, cast on with MC and work ribbing by alternating 5 rows of MC and 3 rows of CC. Work heel flap in 1-row stripes of MC and CC. Then work heel turn all in MC. For foot, again alternate 5 rows of MC and 3 rows of CC. Work toes by alternating 1 row of MC and 1 row of CC. You can easily run colors along on inside of sock without having to cut yarn with each color change.

Baby socks in University of Tennessee colors

Toe-Up Socks

At first there were cuff-down socks, and while it may have taken us a while to get used to the method of knitting two socks simultaneously on two circular needles, the end result was one of complete freedom from the "second sock syndrome." When I started to knit my sock pairs from the toe up, I tried to remain faithful to my comfort zone of working from the cuff down, really I did! But soon, I realized that knitting toe up is in fact slightly less confusing and my interest perked up. But what finally won me over and what I most love about this method is the fact that you can use up all your yarn. Once the foot is done and the heel is turned, you can knit your leg, and knit and knit until the yarn is gone. Knitting without waste! Now that is awesome!

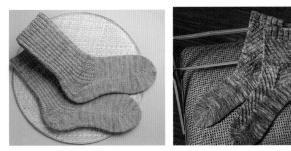

PAGE 44

PAGE 54

PAGE 60

PAGE 66

PAGE 72

PAGE 78

PAGE 82

PAGE 86

Women's Basic Toe-Up Socks

For the basic toe-up pattern, I used Classy, a fabulous hand-dyed, superwash, light worsted-weight yarn by a company with the great name of Dream in Color. Classy, an Australian yarn, is one of the softest washable 100%-superfine-merino wools I've ever worked with, and when you decide to give it a try, you'll be hard pressed to buy just one color because they're all luscious, making a choice near impossible! But no matter what yarn you select for your first toe-up socks, the most important thing is to have fun exploring new knitting avenues. Have fun going down this little windy road.

Skill level: Easy ◖■□◻◻

Sizes: Women's Small (Medium, Large)
To fit shoe sizes: 5–7 (8–9½, 10–12)

MATERIALS

1 (1, 2) skeins of Classy from Dream in Color (100% superfine Australian merino superwash; 4 oz; 250 yds) in color Beach Fog (VM210) **⟨3⟩**

2 size 5 (3.75 mm) circular needles (16" and 24")

Point protectors

2 lockable stitch markers

4 stitch markers

Tapestry needle

GAUGE

6 sts = 1" in St st

JUDY'S MAGIC CAST ON

I learned about Judy and her cast-on technique from a customer when I began working on toe-up socks. It was one of several cast ons that I tried and it was the best by far. Judy Becker is an avid knitter; you can read her blog at www.persistentillusion.com.

CO 16 sts (8 sts per needle) using Judy's magic cast on as follows. (Left-handed knitters please note: you must cast on exactly as shown. Don't be tempted to hold the yarn and needles with the opposite hands.)

1. Pull end from 1 ball of yarn, leaving 10" tail, make sl knot and place it on 24" needle. Hold needles in your right hand, with 24" needle (needle 2) on top of 16" needle (needle 1). Squeeze your thumb and index finger of your left hand together and spread remaining 3 fingers straight out. Sl thumb and index finger (still squeezed together) between the two strands of yarn so that tail hangs over index finger and working yarn hangs over thumb. Grab the 2 strands of yarn, which are lying across your palm, with remaining 3 fingers.

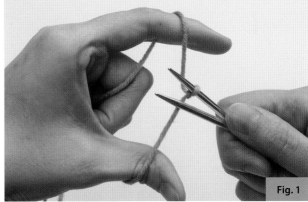
Fig. 1

2. Open your thumb and index finger to form a "C" and tilt them a tad toward you so that index finger sits slightly above thumb. The needle tips sit between both in the middle and face toward your left hand. Now move both needles together upward so that needle 1 (bottom) slides over and behind tail lying across index finger. Guide tail between needles to back and pull newly created st securely around needle 1, but not too tight (fig. 2). Remember, you have to knit it later on.

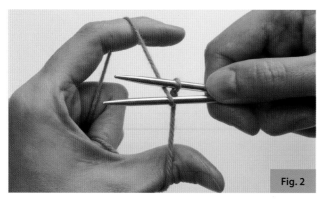

Fig. 2

3. Now move both needles together downward so that needle 2 (top) slips under working yarn lying across thumb, scooping it up to form next st. Guide tail between needles to back and pull newly created st securely around needle 2 (fig. 3). Notice there is 1 st on needle 1 and 2 sts on needle 2.

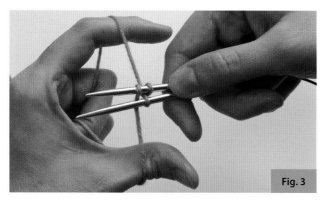

Fig. 3

4. Rep steps 2 and 3, moving needles together first up and over, wrapping tail around needle 1 (bottom needle around top strand); and then down, wrapping working yarn around needle 2 (top needle around bottom strand), until 16 sts total have been CO (8 sts per needle) (fig. 4).

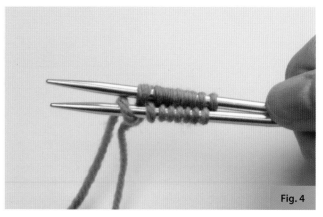

Fig. 4

After the first sock is cast on, your work should look like this.

5. Slide sts to right and toward cables so they remain on needle, but at same time make room for you to CO second sock. With new ball of yarn, CO total of 16 sts (8 sts per needle) for sock 2 as for sock 1 (fig. 5).

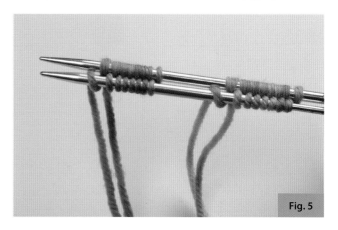

Fig. 5

6. Hold needles in your left hand. Notice that tails and working yarn are facing you. Move them so that the 16" needle ends up sitting on top by letting the 24" needle "roll" forward and down between your fingers. The tips are facing right, and tails and working yarn are behind your work (fig. 6). You'll begin with 16" needle, and sock you CO last becomes first one you'll knit. The 16" needle marks beg of rnd.

Fig. 6

7. Place point protector on each end of 24" needle. Pull end of 24" needle to right and down so that sts sitting on it slide onto cable. The tail is attached to 16" needle and working yarn is attached to 24" needle. Hold tail along with needle in your left hand so that first st can't unravel. It should lie across working yarn. With your

right hand, PU empty end of 16" needle and get ready to knit your first row (half of first rnd) (fig. 7).

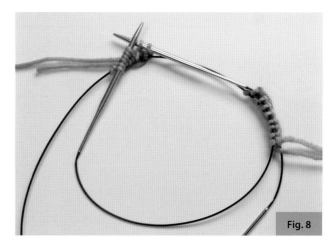

Fig. 7

Tightly knit 8 sts of sock 1. Notice how needle position has changed after you've worked first 8 sts. The two needles are no longer parallel; instead both tips of 16" needle are facing each other. This is an excellent reminder that you have not yet completed row and that you still have to work 8 toe sts for sock 2.

Let sock 1 rest and make sure working yarn hangs behind 16" needle as well as behind and over cable of 24" needle. Scoot toe sts of sock 2 close to needle tip and tightly knit across them (fig. 8).

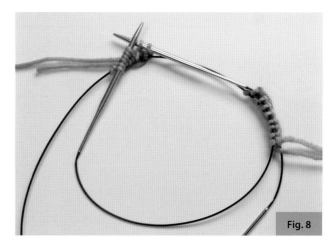

Fig. 8

You've just completed 1 row or first half of rnd for your socks. The needles have opened up and lie parallel once again. To start second row of first rnd, turn your work; tails and working yarn are facing you. Hold needles in left hand and "roll" them so that 16" needle falls backward and 24" needle comes up in front to sit on top. Tails and working yarn are behind work.

8. Switch point protectors if needed, slide sts on 16" needle to its cable, and scoot sts on 24" needle to its tip. *Notice that working yarn is attached to 16" needle and that sts sitting on 24" needle are twisted (facing right).* Switch balls of yarn as you switch socks and knit across first set of sts on 24" needle through *back loop.*

Notice how tips face each other after you've worked first set of sts. Remember that you're only done with half of this row. You still have to knit across sts of sock 2 before row is complete. Once needles are parallel again, turn work; holding needles in your left hand, move 16" needle above 24" needle. Remember to switch point protectors to appropriate needle tips. You're now ready to start first row of next rnd with 16" needle.

Toe Increases

After the CO and untwisting of sts, we're ready to start the toe inc. Beg with 16" needle. Make sure RS faces you at all times as you inc toe. Move working needle on top of resting needle and switch point protectors to appropriate needle tips. Knit rather tightly while working inc rows, otherwise you may end up with tiny holes.

All Sizes

Rnd 1

Rows 1 (16") and 2 (24"): K1, M1R, knit to last st, M1L, K1, rep for sock 2. Turn. (20 sts per sock)

Rnd 2

Rows 1 and 2: Knit even across both socks.

Right Side and Wrong Side of Toe Stitches

The toes of your socks are still tiny, but look at the itty-bitty swatches on your needles. After you're done knitting several rows and you turn and move the needles from your right to your left hand, the wrong sides of the knitted fabric will face you initially. Notice the purl bumps and the working yarn, which is still attached to the top needle. In order to work on the right side of your socks, remember to move the needle you're about to use to the top so it sits above the one you just finished working with. You also never work the needle that has the working yarn attached to it but always the one without!

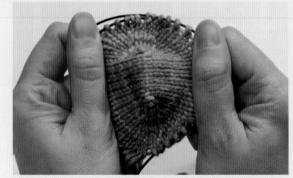

Right side

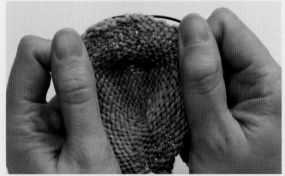

Wrong side

Rnd 3

Rows 1 and 2: K1, M1R, knit to last st, M1L, K1, rep for sock 2. Turn. (24 sts per sock)

Rnd 4

Rows 1 and 2: Knit even across both socks.

Rnds 5 and 6: Rep rnds 3 and 4 once. (28 sts per sock)

Position of Working and Resting Needles

As you get ready to work the next row, switch needles into your left hand as usual, with tips facing to the right. Instead of moving the working needle to sit on top of the resting needle as before, align the tips and hold the resting needle slightly behind the working needle. As before, pull the back needle to the right and down so its stitches slip onto the cable. From now on, the working needle will sit closest to you and in front of the resting needle.

Working needle sits in front of resting needle.

Rnd 7

Rows 1 and 2: K1, M1R, knit to last st, M1L, K1. Rep for sock 2. Turn. (32 sts per sock)

Rnds 8 and 9

Rows 1 and 2: Knit even across both socks.

Rnd 10

Rows 1 and 2: K1, M1R, knit to last st, M1L, K1. Rep for sock 2. Turn. (36 sts per sock)

Rnds 11 and 12

Rows 1 and 2: Knit even across both socks.

Rnd 13

Rows 1 and 2: K1, M1R, knit to last st, M1L, K1. Rep for sock 2. Turn. (40 sts per sock for Small)

Medium and Large

Rnds 14 and 15

Rows 1 and 2: Knit even across both socks.

Rnd 16

Rows 1 and 2: K1, M1R, knit to last st, M1L, K1. Rep for sock 2. Turn. (44 sts per sock)

Large

Rnds 17 and 18

Rows 1 and 2: Knit even across both socks.

Rnd 19

Rows 1 and 2: K1, M1R, knit to last st, M1L, K1. Rep for sock 2. Turn. (48 sts per sock)

All Sizes

Toes should measure approx 1½ (2, 2½)".

FOOT

Fig. 9

Fig. 10

However, it's not always possible to try the sock on. In this case, knit even in rnds until foot measures approx 7 (7½, 8)" from tip of cast-on toe.

EASY HEEL FLAPS

The heel flap is worked back and forth in rows on 16" needle only (half of the sts per sock). Switch point protectors to 24" needle.

Unless otherwise specified, sl all sts pw.

Row 1 (RS): Sl 1 wyif, knit to end. Rep for sock 2.

Row 2 (WS): Sl 1 wyif, purl to last st, K1. Rep for sock 2.

Rep rows 1 and 2 until work measures approx 8¾ (9½, 10)" from tip of toe, or until heel flap reaches back of your heel (fig. 10).

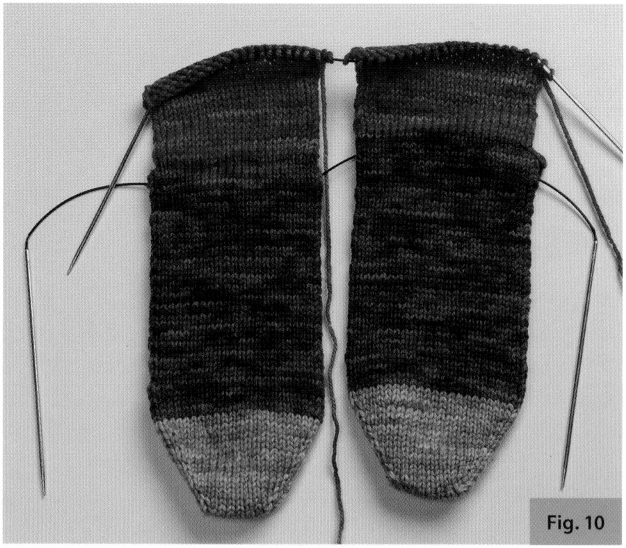

HEEL TURNS

Heel is turned with short rows, which means that you're going to work back and forth within a row rather than finishing it. This technique will leave unworked sts on needle, and both heels cannot be worked at same time. Therefore each heel has to be worked separately. For explanation of italicized instructions in heel turn, see page 16.

Sock 1

All Sizes

Row 1 (RS): Sl 1 wyif, K10 (12, 12), K2tog, K1, turn.

Row 2 (WS): Sl 1 wyif, P3 (5, 3) ssp, P1, turn.

Small and Large

Row 3: Sl 1 *kw wyib*, (K1, sl 1) twice, K2tog, K1, turn.

Row 4: Sl 1 wyif, P5, ssp, P1, turn.

Row 5: Sl 1 kw wyib, K2, (sl 1, K1) twice, K2tog, K1, turn.

Row 6: Sl 1 wyif, P7, ssp, P1, turn.

Row 7: Sl 1 kw wyib, (K1, sl 1) 4 times, K2tog, K1, turn.

Small

Row 8: Sl 1 wyif, P9, ssp, K1, turn.

Row 9: Sl 1 *pw wyif*, K2, (sl 1, K1) 4 times, K1. *Do not turn.* (12 sts rem)

Large

Row 8: Sl 1 wyif, P9, ssp, P1, turn.

Row 9: Sl 1 kw wyib, K2, (sl 1, K1) 4 times, K2tog, K1, turn.

Row 10: Sl 1 wyif, P11, ssp, K1, turn.

Row 11: Sl 1 *pw wyif*, (K1, sl 1) 6 times, K1. *Do not turn.* (14 sts rem)

Medium

Row 3: Sl 1 *kw wyib*, (K1, sl 1) 3 times, K2tog, K1, turn.

Row 4: Sl 1 wyif, P7, ssp, P1, turn.

Row 5: Sl 1 kw wyib, K2, (sl 1, K1) 3 times, K2tog, K1, turn

Row 6: Sl 1 wyif, P9, ssp, P1, turn.

Row 7: Sl 1 kw wyib, (K1, sl 1) 5 times, K2tog, K1, turn.

Row 8: Sl 1 wyif, P11, ssp, K1, turn.

Row 9: Sl 1 *pw wyif*, K2, (sl 1, K1) 5 times, K1. *Do not turn.* (14 sts rem)

All Sizes

The first heel is turned. *Do not turn second heel just yet.*

Cont with same needle tip, pm, and PU 11 (13, 13) sts along side of heel flap, PU 1 more st in gusset corner for total of 12 (14, 14) sts. (See "Closing the Gusset Gap" on page 15)

Sock 2

Before you beg on second heel, notice that tips of your 16" needle are facing each other; this row is only half completed. Move sock 1 off RH needle and onto cable. PU needle that holds second heel flap in your left hand and turn heel as for sock 1.

You've just turned second heel; 12 (14, 14) sts rem. Cont with same needle tip and PU 11 (13, 13) sts along side of heel flap, PU 1 more gusset st in corner as before for total of 12 (14, 14) sts (fig. 11).

Fig. 11

Turn your work so that instep sts are facing you. [20 (22, 24) sts per sock] Switch point protectors to 16" needle. With 24" needle, knit even across all instep sts for both socks.

Remember to tighten working yarn after having knit second st and to push worked sts of sock 1 back onto cable before continuing with sock 2. Turn.

The heel sts are facing you once again. Switch point protectors to 24" needle. PU and knit gusset sts on second side of your socks, this time starting in gusset corner and working up heel flap. With your left hand grab heel flap you're getting ready to work, with your right hand pick up RH (empty) needle tip of 16" needle. The working yarn should be ready and waiting in corner of gusset of this sock (fig. 12).

PU 1 gusset st in corner as before. Pull working yarn tight and cont to PU 11 (13, 13) sts along side of heel flap for total of 12 (14, 14) sts, pm. Knit even across 12 (14, 14) heel sts, pm, knit across gusset sts on other side of heel flap. Push sock 1 off RH needle and onto cable. Rep for sock 2.

Both heels are turned and all gusset sts have been picked up. You should have 2 st markers in place per sock—1 at each side of heel sts to help you check your gusset dec and stay in pattern (fig. 13). From now on, you'll once again knit in rows as well as rnds. If you still need help remembering, cont to switch point protectors to tips of resting needle. Turn your work so that instep sts are facing you and knit across them. There are 36 (42, 42) sts on 16" needle and 20 (22, 24) sts on 24" needle.

Fig. 12

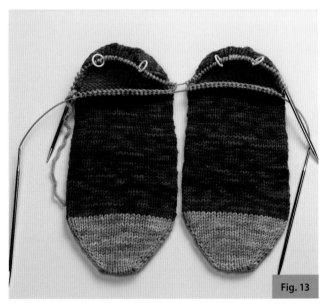

Fig. 13

GUSSET DECREASES

From now on you'll knit even across instep sts on 24" needle and dec gusset sts on 16" needle until there are once again 20 (22, 24) sts per heel.

Sl markers as you come to them.

Rnd 1

Row 1 (heel): Knit to first marker, sl 0 (0, 1), (K1, sl 1) 6 (7, 6) times, K0 (0, 1), knit to last 3 sts, K2tog, K1. Rep for sock 2.

Row 2 (instep): Knit even across instep sts of both socks.

Rnd 2

Row 1 (heel): K1, ssk, knit to end of sock 1. Rep for sock 2.

Row 2 (instep): Knit even across instep sts of both socks.

Rep rnds 1 and 2 until 20 (22, 24) sts rem per sock on 16" needle.

Perfect Gusset Triangle (optional): See page 16. Dec as follows, removing markers as you come to them.

Row 1 (heel): K1, ssk, K2, M1L, K10 (12, 14), M1R, K2, K2tog, K1. Rep for sock 2.

Row 2 (instep): Knit even across both socks.

LEGS

The 16" needle marks beg of rnd.

Knit 1 rnd even across both needles.

Beg leg patt.

Rnd 1

Rows 1 and 2: (K1, P1) across all sts of both socks.

Rnd 2

Rows 1 and 2: Knit even across all sts of both socks.

Rep rnds 1 and 2 until patterned leg measures 6" or until desired length.

CUFFS

Work (K1, P1) ribbing (fig. 14) (rnd 1 of leg only) for another 2".

Fig. 14

BO each sock using sewn BO on page 13. Weave in all ends and try your socks on *immediately*. You can also try them on first and weave in your ends later . . . instant gratification!

In the Diagonal

So I jumped on the Flat Feet band wagon—because the yarn is so cool! If you're not familiar with Flat Feet, let me introduce you to the latest craze in sock knitting.

Flat Feet yarn doesn't come in balls or skeins, it comes in flats (see photo bottom right)—pieces of machine-knitted fabric that are hand-dyed after they've been knitted. You unravel the knitted swatches as you knit your socks, thus creating unique color patterns as you work your socks. Because each Flat Feet swatch is unique, no two pairs of socks are identical—even from the same colorway.

This yarn is not everybody's cup of tea, especially since it's all crinkled as you unravel the piece, though I can vouch for the fact that any uneven stitch work will disappear after the first blocking or washing. Since Flat Feet yarn is hand-dyed, some sheets will bleed more than others. You can either rinse the sheets in cold water and a little vinegar before use, or wash and block the finished socks before wearing them to avoid dyeing your feet.

I had a great time knitting socks while unraveling a preknitted swatch. It definitely gives a whole new meaning to the term "frogging" (unknitting)! But don't just take my word for it, go ahead and give it a try yourself.

Skill level: Intermediate ◖■■■◗

Sizes: Women's Small (Medium, Large)
To fit shoe sizes: 5–6 (7–9, 10–11)

MATERIALS

1 flat of Flat Feet from Conjoined Creations (80% superwash merino, 20% nylon; 100 g; approx 400 yds) in color Bright Kaleidoscope **❶**

2 size 2 circular needles (16" and 24")

Cable needle (optional)

Point protectors

5 lockable stitch markers

4 stitch markers

Tapestry needle

GAUGE

7½ sts = 1" in St st

Sheets of Flat Feet (in the color called Bright Kaleidoscope) as they are unraveled

SPECIAL INSTRUCTIONS

T2B (Twist 2 Back)

With cable needle: Sl next st onto cn and hold at back, K1, P1 from cn.

Without cable needle: Knit into front of second st on LH needle, then purl first st, sl both sts off needle at same time.

T2F (Twist 2 Front)

With cable needle: Sl next st onto cn and hold at front, P1, K1 from cn.

Without cable needle: Purl into back of second st on LH needle, then knit first st, sl both sts off needle at same time.

TOES

Referring to "Judy's Magic Cast On" on page 45, CO and set up 20 sts per sock (10 sts per half). The 16" needle marks beg of rnd.

Basic Rnd

Row 1 (16" needle): Knit even across all sts.

Row 2 (24" needle): All sts on this needle are twisted and need to be knit tbl.

Inc Rnds

Only rnds are shown below. For every rnd, you'll work same instructions on 16" needle and 24" needle. See page 17.

All Sizes

Rnd 1: K1, M1R, knit to last st, M1L, K1. Rep for sock 2. (24 sts per sock)

Rnd 2: Knit even across both socks.

Rnd 3: K1, M1R, knit to last st, M1L, K1. Rep for sock 2. (28 sts per sock)

Rnd 4: Knit even across both socks.

Rep rnds 3 and 4 twice more. (36 sts per sock)

Rnd 9: K1, M1R, knit to last st, M1L, K1. Rep for sock 2. (40 sts per sock)

Rnds 10 and 11: Knit even across both socks.

Small

Rep rnds 9–11 a total of 3 more times, then rnd 9 once more. (56 sts per sock)

Toe should measure approx 2" from tip.

Medium

Rep rnds 9–11 a total of 4 more times, then rnd 9 once more. (60 sts per sock)

Toe should measure approx 2¼" from tip.

Large

Rep rnds 9–11 a total of 5 more times, then rnd 9 once more. (64 sts per sock)

Toe should measure approx 2½" from tip.

Small and Large: Knit 1 rnd.

Medium: Knit 1 rnd and evenly inc 2 sts on 24" needle only.

FOOT

Before beg diagonal patt, mark second sock with lockable st marker or piece of yarn; leave first sock plain. For opposing diagonals, each sock has different pattern sequence within a row; therefore they will be referred to as *marked* and *plain* to avoid confusion.

Diagonal Patt

Rnd 1

NOTE: Row 1 (sole sts) in all rnds: Knit even across all sts.

Row 2 (marked): *P2, T2B, rep from * to end.

Row 2 (plain): *P2, T2F, rep from * to end.

Rnd 2

Row 2 (marked): P2, K1, *P3, K1, rep from * to last st, P1.

Row 2 (plain): K1, *P3, K1, rep from * to end.

Rnd 3

Row 2 (marked): P1, *T2B, P2, rep from * to last 3 sts, T2B, P1.

Row 2 (plain): P3, T2F, *P2, T2F, rep from * to last 3 sts, P3.

Rnd 4

Row 2 (marked): P1, K1, *P3, K1, rep from * to last 2 sts, P2.

Row 2 (plain): K1, *P3, K1, rep from * to last 3 sts, P3.

Rnd 5

Row 2 (marked): *T2B, P2, rep from * to end.

Row 2 (plain): *T2F, P2, rep from * to end.

Rnd 6

Row 2 (marked): *K1, P3, rep from * to end.

Row 2 (plain): P1, K1, *P3, K1, rep from * to last 2 sts, P2.

Rnd 7

Row 2 (marked): P3, *T2B, P2, rep from * to last st, K1.

Row 2 (plain): P1, *T2F, P2, rep from * to last 3 sts, T2F, P1.

Rnd 8

Row 2 (marked): *P3, K1, rep from * to end.

Row 2 (plain): P2, K1, *P3, K1 to last st, P1.

Rep rnds 1–8 until foot measures approx 7 (7½, 8)" from tip of toe or until it reaches beg of your ankle when tried on. End with rnd 8.

EASY HEEL FLAPS

The heel flap is worked back and forth in rows on 16" needle only.

Unless otherwise specified, sl all sts pw.

Row 1 (RS): Sl 1 wyif, knit to end. Rep for sock 2.

Row 2 (WS): Sl 1 wyif, purl to last st, K1. Rep for sock 2.

Rep rows 1 and 2 until work measures approx 8¾ (9½, 10)" from tip of toe, or until heel flap reaches back of your heel.

HEEL TURNS

The heel is turned with short rows; therefore each heel is worked separately, beg with sock 1. Cont to work in rows and with same needle as for heel flap. For explanation of italicized instructions in heel turn, see page 16.

Sock 1

All Sizes

Row 1 (RS): Sl 1 wyif, K14 (16, 16), K2tog, K1, turn.

Row 2 (WS): Sl 1 wyif, P3 (5, 3) ssp, P1, turn.

Row 3: Sl 1 *kw wyib*, (K1, sl 1) 2 (3, 2) times, K2tog, K1, turn.

Row 4: Sl 1 wyif, P5 (7, 5), ssp, P1, turn.

Row 5: Sl 1 kw wyib, K2, (sl 1, K1) 2 (3, 2) times, K2tog, K1, turn.

Row 6: Sl 1 wyif, P7 (9, 7), ssp, P1, turn.

Row 7: Sl 1 kw wyib, (K1, sl 1) 4 (5, 4) times, K2tog, K1, turn.

Row 8: Sl 1 wyif, P9 (11, 9), ssp, P1, turn.

Row 9: Sl 1 kw wyib, K2, (sl 1, K1) 4 (5, 4) times, K2tog, K1, turn.

Row 10: Sl 1 wyif, P11 (13, 11), ssp, P1 turn.

Row 11: Sl 1 kw wyib, (K1, sl 1) 6 (7, 6) times, K2tog, K1, turn.

Small Only

Row 12: Sl 1 wyif, P13, ssp, K1, turn.

Row 13: Sl 1 *pw wyif*, K2, (sl 1, K1) 6 times, K1, *do not turn.* (16 sts rem)

Medium Only

Row 12: Sl 1, P15, ssp, K1, turn.

Row 13: Sl 1 *pw wyif*, K2, (sl 1, K) 7 times, K1, *do not turn.* (18 sts rem)

Large Only

Row 12: Sl 1, P13, ssp, P1, turn.

Row 13: Sl 1 kw wyib, K2, (sl 1, K1) 6 times, K2tog, K1, turn.

Row 14: Sl 1 wyif, P15, ssp, K1, turn.

Row 15: Sl 1 *pw wyif*, (K1, sl 1) 8 times, K1, *do not turn.* (18 sts rem)

All Sizes

Cont with same needle tip, PU 16 (18, 18) sts along heel flap of heel just turned, PU 1 gusset st in corner (see "Closing the Gusset Gap" on page 15) for total of 17 (19, 19) sts.

Sock 2

Move sock to cable and turn heel for sock 2 same as sock 1. After second heel is turned, cont with same needle tip, PU 16 (18, 18) sts along heel flap, PU 1 gusset st in corner for total of 17 (19, 19) sts. Turn. If necessary, switch point protectors to appropriate needle. Cont in diagonal patt as est and work across both socks on 24" needle. Turn.

Beg at gusset corner of first sock, *PU 1 gusset st in corner, then PU 16 (18, 18) sts along second side of heel flap for total of 17 (19, 19) sts. Pm, knit in est K1, sl 1 patt across 16 (18, 18) heel sts, pm, knit across gusset sts on other side. Rep from * for sock 2, beg in gusset corner. Turn. Work in diagonal patt as est across both socks on 24" needle.

Both heels are turned and all gusset sts have been picked up. From now on, you'll once again knit in rows as well as rnds. If you still need help remembering, cont to switch point protectors to tips of resting needle. There are 50 (56, 56) sts on 16" needle and 28 (32, 32) sts on 24" needle.

GUSSET DECREASES

Only heel sts are dec. Sl markers as you come to them.

Rnd 1

Row 1 (heel): Knit to first marker, (K1, sl 1) 8 (9, 9) times, knit to last 3 sts, K2tog, K1. Rep for sock 2.

Row 2 (instep): Work diagonal patt as est across both socks.

Rnd 2

Row 1 (heel): K1, ssk, knit even to end. Rep for sock 2.

Row 2 (instep): Work diagonal patt as est across both socks.

Rep rnds 1 and 2 until 28 (32, 32) heel sts are left per sock, matching number of instep sts for total of 56 (64, 64) sts per sock.

Perfect Gusset Triangle (optional): See page 16. Dec as follows, removing markers as you come to them.

Row 1 (heel): K1, ssk, knit to marker, M1L, knit to next marker, M1R, knit to last 3 sts, K2tog, K1. Rep for sock 2.

Row 2 (instep): Knit even across both socks.

LEGS

See sidebar below.

Note that 24" needle marks beg (row 1) of rnd from now on.

Work in patt as est across both socks (first marked then plain sock) on 24" needle. Turn. Cont in diagonal patt until leg measures approx 3" or until desired length.

CUFFS

Work in K1, P1 for 1½". BO loosely using sewn BO on page 13.

Working Diagonal Pattern in the Round for Legs

From now on, diagonal patt wraps around leg upward in rnds and alternates between twist and knit row. The sts are forever moving and there is no longer set row rep.

To help you remember, note which twist (T2F or T2B) belongs to which sock (marked or plain). Cont in patt as est on previous rnd. Start 16" needle with plain sock; make sure you are following correct twist instructions!

As you work, keep lockable markers handy. Every so often you'll have to sl sts from 1 needle to other in order to accommodate twist, and markers will help you to switch them smoothly. Be sure to move them evenly so that st count per set remains the same. For example, if you sl 2 sts from end of 16" needle to beg of 24" needle, you'll have to sl 2 sts from end of 24" needle to beg of 16" needle. Just work the patt a while; you'll see how easy it is. If you need help, use 8-rnd rep in foot section to guide you.

Wondrous Cable Tree

This particular cable pattern, worked in this particular yarn, is way on top of my list of things to knit for myself. (You didn't actually think I get to wear any of the socks shown in the book, did you?) Be that as it may, I think these socks are simply beautiful and very feminine. (Did I mention I'm a girlie girl, and are you really surprised?)

Skill level: Intermediate ◖■■▭

Sizes: Women's Small (Medium, Large)

To fit shoe sizes: 5–6 (7–9, 10–11)

MATERIALS

2 (2, 3) skeins of Maxime Print from Filatura Di Crosa (80% merino superwash wool, 20% polyamide; 50 g/1.75 oz; 186 yds/170 m) in color 5062 🔢

2 size 2 (2.75 mm) circular needles (16" and 24")

Cable needle (or a 5"-long, size 1 double-pointed needle)

Point protectors

3 lockable stitch markers

1 stitch marker

Tapestry needle

GAUGE

8 sts = 1" in St st.

SPECIAL INSTRUCTIONS

C7F: Sl 3 sts to cn and hold at front, K4, K3 from cn.

TOES

Referring to "Judy's Magic Cast On" on page 45, CO and set up 20 sts for each sock (10 sts per half). The 16" needle marks beg of rnd.

Basic Rnd

Row 1 (16" needle): Knit even across all sts.

Row 2 (24" needle): All sts on this needle are twisted and need to be knit tbl.

Inc Rnds

Only rnds are shown below. For every rnd, you'll work same instructions on 16" needle and 24" needle. See page 16.

All Sizes

Rnd 1: K1, M1R, knit to last st, M1L, K1. Rep for sock 2. (24 sts per sock)

Rnd 2: Knit even across both socks.

Rnd 3: K1, M1R, knit to last st, M1L, K1. Rep for sock 2. (28 sts per sock)

Rnd 4: Knit even across both socks.

Rep rnds 3 and 4 another 2 times. (36 sts per sock)

Rnd 9: K1, M1R, knit to last st, M1L, K1. Rep for sock 2. (40 sts per sock)

Rnds 10 and 11: Knit even across both socks.

Small

Rep rnds 9–11 for 3 more times, then rnd 9 once more. (56 sts per sock)

Toe should measure approx 2" from tip.

Medium

Rep rnds 9–11 for 4 more times, then rnd 9 once more. (60 sts per sock)

Toe should measure approx 2¼" from tip.

Large

Rep rnds 9–11 for 5 more times, then rnd 9 once more. (64 sts per sock)

Toe should measure approx 2½" from tip.

All Sizes

Work foot in St st (knit each rnd) until it measures 6½ (7, 7½)" from tip of toe.

GUSSET INCREASES

The gusset is worked on 16" needle (future heel) only.

Rnd 1

Row 1 (16"): K1, M1L, knit to last st, M1R, K1, rep for sock 2. [30 (32, 34) sts per half sock]

Row 2 (24"): Knit even across all sts.

Rnd 2 and all even-numbered rnds/rows 1 and 2: Knit across both needles.

Rnd 3

Row 1 (16"): K1, M1L, knit to last st, M1R, K1, rep for sock 2. [32 (34, 36) sts per half sock]

Row 2 (24"): Knit even across all sts.

Rep rnds 2 and 3 until 4 sts per gusset (8 sts total/per sock) have been inc on 16" needle. End with an inc rnd on 16" needle. [36 (38, 40) sts per half sock]

SHORT-ROW HEELS

The short-row heel (see page 12) is worked back and forth in rows on 16" needle only. Place point protectors on resting one before you beg.

Unless otherwise specified, sl all st pw.

Sock 1

Row 1 (16") (RS): Knit to last st, w&t.

Row 2 (16") (WS): Purl to last st, w&t.

Row 3: Knit to last 2 sts, w&t.

Row 4: Purl to last 2 sts, w&t.

Row 5: Knit to last 3 sts, w&t.

Row 6: Purl to last 3 sts, w&t.

Row 7: Knit to last 4 sts, w&t.

Row 8: Purl to last 4 sts, w&t.

Cont to work w&t patt, wrapping 1 new st in each row until total of 12 (13, 13) sts have been wrapped on both sides. [12 (12, 14) sts rem unwrapped in middle section] This is first part of short-row heel.

Unwrapping Short Rows

Row 1 (RS):

Small: (K1, ssk) twice, (K2tog, K1) twice to reach first wrapped st. (4 sts have been dec)

Medium: K1, ssk, knit to last 3 sts before first wrapped st, K2tog, K1. (2 sts have been dec)

Large: (K1, ssk) twice, K2, (K2tog, K1) twice to reach first wrapped st. (4 sts have been dec).

All Sizes

There should be 32 (36, 36) sts rem per half sock on 16" needle.

Wyib and RH needle, PU wrap on LH needle by slipping it from bottom up through wrap. Leave wrap sitting on RH needle and knit the st that was wrapped;

pass wrap over st and off needle like psso. Next st w&t (it will now be wrapped twice).

Row 2 (WS): Purl to first wrapped st, with wyif and RH needle, PU wrap on RS (facing away from you) from bottom up. Leave wrap sitting on RH needle and purl the st that was wrapped; pass wrap over st and off needle. Next st, w&t (it will now be wrapped twice).

From now on, you'll PU 2 wraps for each st, work and pass wraps over st and off needle.

Row 3: Knit to first wrapped st, with wyib and RH needle, PU wraps and leave on RH needle; knit the st that was wrapped; pass wraps over st and off needle. Next st, w&t.

Rep rows 2 and 3 until all (double) wrapped sts have been worked, ending with row 2.

Knit even across heel sts of sock 1 and slide to cable. Work short-row heel for sock 2, ending with row 2. Turn work so RH side of sock 2 is facing you once again, and knit across its heel sts. Turn.

Note that each sock has more heel than instep sts at this point. Don't panic! We'll add to the instep to even them out again.

Instep sts are facing you: PU 2 sts in gusset corner, knit to end of sock 1, PU 2 sts in gusset corner. Rep for sock 2. [32 (34, 36) sts per instep]

LEGS

Heel sts are facing you and 16" needle marks beg of rnd.

Instep Increases

Rnd 1

Row 1: Knit even across both socks.

Row 2: K12, M0 (1, 0), K12, M0 (1, 0), knit to end of sock 1. Rep for sock 2. [32 (36, 36) sts per instep for total of 64 (72, 72) sts per sock]

Rnds 2 and 3: Knit even across both needles.

Cable Pattern

Beg cable patt, following chart on facing page.

To cont cable into cuff, leg has to be worked to rnd 3 or 19.

Rep cable patt twice.

Small and Medium: Work rnds 1–3 once more (total of 67 rnds).

Large: Work rnds 1–19 once more (total of 83 rnds).

CUFFS

Small

Rnds 1–7: K1, P3, K7, P3, K3, P3, K7, P3, K2. Rep for sock 2.

Rnd 8: K1, P3, C7F, P3, K3, P3, C7F, P3, K2. Rep for sock 2.

Rnds 9–15: Rep rnd 1.

Rnd 16: Rep rnd 8.

Rnd 17: Rep rnd 1.

Medium and Large

Rnd 1: P1, K2tog, K1, P2, K7, P2, K2, P2, K1, K2tog, P2, K7, P2, K2, P1. Rep for sock 2.

Rnds 2–7: P1, K2, P2, K7, (P2, K2) twice, P2, K7, P2, K2, P1. Rep for sock 2.

Rnd 8: P1, K2, P2, C7F, (P2, K2) twice, P2, C7F, P2, K2, P1. Rep for sock 2.

Rnds 9–15: Rep rnd 2.

Rnd 16: Rep rnd 8.

Rnd 17: Rep rnd 2.

All Sizes

BO socks using sewn BO on page 13.

Row numbers (right side, top to bottom): 32, 31, 30, 29, 28, 27, 26, 25, 24, 23, 22, 21, 20, 19, 18, 17, 16, 15, 14, 13, 12, 11, 10, 9, 8, 7, 6, 5, 4, 3, 2, 1

Key

☐ K	⋁ K1 tbl	
— P	⋌ K3tog	
○ YO	⋋ K3tog tbl	
╱ K2tog	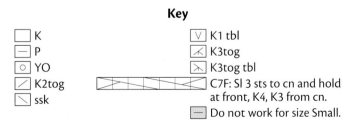 C7F: Sl 3 sts to cn and hold at front, K4, K3 from cn.	
╲ ssk	▦ Do not work for size Small.	

Robin's "Cute" Fair Isle Socks

My friend Robin is a lovely person who is still relatively new to knitting. Recently, she walked into the shop in utter bewilderment. "I have a question," she said. "You know how you taught me that if I work with multiple colors, I have to cut the yarn when I change to a new one?" I nodded, thinking about stripes.

"Well," she continued, "I was studying a Fair Isle pattern yesterday, and it changes color with every stitch."

"Hmm," I said.

"So how is that supposed to work?" She asked.

I looked at her. "What do you mean?"

"How can I knit one and cut, knit one and cut, and keep it from falling apart? Do I knot each tail together with the next or what? I don't understand."

For a few seconds, I stood there staring at her; then I smiled and said, "Oh Robin, you're so cute!" I explained the workings of Fair Isle to her, and ever since that day she insists that when I say cute, I'm just being nice and "cute" really translates into dumb . . . now isn't that cute?

Skill level: Intermediate ■■■□

Sizes: Women's Small (Medium, Large)

To fit shoe sizes: 5–6 (7–9, 10–11)

MATERIALS

MC 2 skeins of Gems Super Fine Fingering Weight from Louet (100% superfine merino wool; 50 g; 185 yds) in color 1542 (teal) (1)

CC 2 skeins of Gems Super Fine Fingering Weight from Louet in color 1262 (crabapple blossom)

2 size 2 (2.75 mm) circular needles (16" and 24")

Point protectors

2 lockable stitch markers

1 stitch marker

Tapestry needle

GAUGE

7 sts = 1" in St st

TOES

With CC and referring to "Judy's Magic Cast On" on page 45, CO and set up 16 sts per sock (8 sts per half). The 16" needle marks beg of rnd.

Basic Rnd

Row 1 (16" needle): Knit even across all sts.

Row 2 (24" needle): All sts on this needle are twisted and need to be knit tbl.

Inc Rnds

Only rnds are shown below. For every rnd, you'll work same instructions on 16" needle and 24" needle. See page 17.

All Sizes

Rnd 1: K1, M1R, knit to last st, M1L, K1. Rep for sock 2. (20 sts per sock)

Rnd 2: Knit even across both socks.

Rnd 3: K1, M1R, knit to last st, M1L, K1. Rep for sock 2. (24 sts per sock)

Rnd 4: Knit even across both socks.

Rep rnds 3 and 4 another 3 times. (36 sts per sock)

Rnd 11: K1, M1R, knit to last st, M1L, K1. Rep for sock 2. (40 sts per sock)

Rnds 12 and 13: Knit even across both socks.

Small

Work rnds 11–13 another 3 times and rnd 11 once more. (56 sts per sock)

Medium

Work rnds 11–13 another 4 times and rnd 11 once more. (60 sts per sock)

Large

Work rnds 11–13 another 5 times and rnd 11 once more. (64 sts per sock)

All Sizes

Toes should measure approx 2 (2⅛", 2¼") from tip. Knit 1 rnd even across both needles. Cut CC.

FOOT

Stripe Pattern

All Sizes

Rnds 1–10: With MC, knit even across both needles. Do not cut yarn.

Rnds 11 and 12: With CC, knit even across both needles. Cut yarn.

Rnds 13–18: With MC, knit even across both needles. Do not cut yarn.

Rnds 19 and 20: With CC, knit even across both needles. Cut yarn.

Rnds 21–29: With MC, knit even across both needles.

Rnd 30: Evenly inc 4 (10, 6) sts per sock; 2 (5, 3) sts per half as follows.

> **Small:** K10, (M1, K9) twice, rep for sock 2. (60 sts per sock)
>
> **Medium:** K5, (M1, K5) 5 times, rep for sock 2. (70 sts per sock)
>
> **Large:** K8, (M1, K8) 3 times, rep for sock 2. (70 sts per sock)

Fair Isle Pattern

Follow rnds 7–12 on Fair Isle chart once (see page 71).

Cut CC and cont with MC in stripe patt, knit even across both needles for 1 rnd.

Rnd 2: Evenly dec 4 (10, 6) sts per sock; 2 (5, 3) sts per half as follows.

Small: K9, K2tog, K8, K2tog, K9, rep for sock 2. (56 sts per sock)

Medium: K5, (K2tog, K4) 5 times, rep for sock 2. (60 sts per sock)

Large: K8, (K2tog, K7) 3 times, rep for sock 2. (64 sts per sock)

All Sizes

Rnds 3–12: Knit even across both needles. Do not cut yarn.

Rnds 13 and 14: With CC, knit even across both needles. Cut yarn.

Cont with MC and knit even in rnds until foot measures approx 6½ (7, 7½)" from tip of toe.

In the last rnd dec 0 (4, 4) sts per sock, 0 (2, 2) sts per half. [56 (56, 60) sts rem per sock.]

GUSSET INCREASES

The inc is worked on 16" needle (future heel) only.

Cont with MC.

Rnd 1

Row 1 (16"): K1, M1L, knit to last st, M1R, K1. Rep for sock 2. [30 (30 32) sts per half sock]

Row 2 (24"): Knit even across both needles.

Rnd 2 and all even-numbered rnds: Knit even across both needles.

Rnd 3

Row 1: K1, M1L, knit to last st, M1R, K1. Rep for sock 2. [32 (32, 34) sts per half sock]

Row 2: Knit even across both needles.

Rep rnds 2 and 3 until 4 sts per gusset (8 sts total/per sock) have been inc on 16" needle. End with inc rnd. [36 (36, 38) sts per half sock]

SHORT-ROW HEELS

The short-row heel (see page 12) is worked back and forth in rows on 16" needle only. Place point protectors on resting needle before you beg.

Unless otherwise specified, sl all sts pw.

Change to CC.

Sock 1

Row 1 (RS): Knit to last st, w&t.

Row 2 (WS): Purl to last st, w&t.

Row 3: Knit to last 2 sts, w&t.

Row 4: Purl to last 2 sts, w&t.

Row 5: Knit to last 3 sts, w&t.

Row 6: Purl to last 3 sts, w&t.

Row 7: Knit to last 4 sts, w&t.

Row 8: Purl to last 4 sts, w&t.

Cont to work w&t patt, wrapping 1 new st in each row until total of 12 sts have been wrapped on both sides. [12 (12, 14) sts rem unwrapped in middle section.] This is first part of short-row heel.

Unwrapping Short Rows

Row 1 (RS):

Small and Medium: Ssk 3 times, K2tog 3 times to reach first wrapped st (6 sts have been dec).

Large: (K1, ssk 3) times, K2tog 3 times, K1 to reach first wrapped st (6 sts have been dec).

There should be 30 (30, 32) sts rem per half sock on 16" needle.

All Sizes

Wyib and RH needle, PU wrap on LH needle by slipping it from bottom up through wrap. Leave wrap sitting on RH needle and knit the st that was wrapped; pass wrap over st and off needle like psso. Next st, w&t (it will now be wrapped twice).

Row 2 (WS): Purl to first wrapped st, with wyif and RH needle, PU wrap on RS (facing away from you) from bottom up. Leave wrap sitting on RH needle and purl the st that was wrapped; pass wrap over st and off needle. Next st, w&t (it will now be wrapped twice).

From now on, you'll PU 2 wraps for each st, work and pass wraps over st and off needle.

Row 3: Knit to first wrapped st, with wyib and RH needle, PU wraps and leave on RH needle; knit the st that was wrapped; pass wraps over st and off needle. Next st, w&t.

Rep rows 2 and 3 until all (double) wrapped sts have been worked, ending with row 2. Knit even across sock 1 and slide to cable. Work short-row heel for sock 2. as for sock 1 (ending with a row 2) turn work so RH side of sock 2 is facing you once again. Knit across sock 2 and turn. Knit even across all sts on 24" needle.

Change to MC and knit across heel sts on 16" needle, AT SAME TIME dec 2 (0, 0) sts on each set of heel sts. [28 (30, 32) heel sts per sock] Turn. Knit across 24" needle and inc 0 (2, 2,) sts on each set of instep sts. [28

(30, 32) instep sts per sock for total of 56 (60, 64) sts per sock]

LEGS

Cont with MC and knit even across both needles for 2". Change to CC and knit 1 rnd. Cont with CC and work in K1, P1 ribbing for 2¾", ending with row 2 (24" needle). TURN SOCKS INSIDE OUT.

CUFFS

Beg with 24" needle (working yarn is attached to it!), knit 1 rnd. Do not cut yarn.

Beg Picot Tube

Rnd 1

Row 1: Change to MC and, just as in the easy heel gusset corner (see page 15), PU 1 st. Sl st from RH to LH needle and K2tog. This will close gap created by turning sock inside out and reversing knitting direction. Rep for sock 2.

Row 2: Knit even across both socks.

Rnds 2–4: Knit even across both needles.

Rnd 5: (K2tog, YO) to end of sock 1. Rep for sock 2.

Before you cont, check to make sure you've added YO at end of each set of sts.

Rnds 6–9: Knit even across both needles. [56 (60, 64) sts]

Beg with 24" needle to create picot tube. Have needle tip with sts in LH as if to knit. You may use RH needle tip or small dpn to help you PU sts.

Row 1: On WS, insert RH needle from bottom up into first st of first (row 1) knitted row and pick it up. Trying not to stretch sts too much, use same RH needle and sl first st from LH needle onto it. Now pass first (picked up) st over second (slipped) st and off RH needle; 1 st rem on RH needle. Dive back down to row 1 on WS

and PU next st, move back up to current row and sl a st from LH to RH needle. Now pass picked-up st over slipped st; 2 sts rem on RH needle. Cont in this manner until end of sock 1. Place last worked st on lockable marker. Rep for sock 2.

Row 2: Move st from marker to RH needle and cont to work picot tube across sock 1; sl last worked st on lockable marker. Rep for sock 2. Do not cut yarn.

Change to CC and knit even across both needles.

Inc rnd: Evenly inc 4 (10, 6) sts per sock [2 (5, 3) sts per half] as follows.

Small: Sl st from lockable marker to LH needle, K10, (M1, K9) twice. Rep for sock 2. (60 sts per sock)

Medium: Sl st from lockable marker to LH needle, K5, (M1, K5) 5 times. Rep for sock 2. (70 sts per sock)

Large: Sl st from lockable marker to LH needle, K8, (M1, K8) 3 times. Rep for sock 2. (70 sts per sock)

Work rows 1–24 once from Fair Isle chart at right.

Cut MC and cont with CC, knit even across both needles for 1 rnd.

Rnd 2: Evenly dec total of 4 (10, 6) sts per sock [2 (5, 3) sts per half] as follows.

Small: K9, K2tog, K8, K2tog, K9, rep for sock 2. (56 sts per sock)

Medium: K5, (K2tog, K4) 5 times, rep for sock 2. (60 sts per sock)

Large: K8, (K2tog, K7) 3 times, rep for sock 2. (64 sts per sock)

Beg seed-st patt as follows.

Rnd 1: (K1, P1) across both needles.

Rnd 2: (P1, K1) across both needles.

Rep rnds 1 and 2 until seed-st patt measures about ¼". BO loosely using sewn BO on page 13.

Fair Isle

Key

▨ MC

☐ CC

FALLING LEAVES

I am dedicating this pattern to my good friend Maryann. It was her idea to include at least one sock with a lace pattern. "Oh, let's try," she said innocently and with a certain gleam in her eyes. "I just love this all-around lace pattern." Well, let me tell you this, if you're ready for a challenge, you'll love this pattern too! Ahh, it's indeed very beautiful . . . but don't say I didn't warn you!

Socks made from silk and bamboo blends are heavenly soft and feel luxurious on your feet. Panda Silk by Crystal Palace Yarns is no exception.

Before I forget! You'll be tempted to read through this pattern from beginning to end. Don't! It will only confuse you. In this case, it's best to work line by line without knowing what awaits you down the way.

Skill level: Experienced ◆ ■ ■ ▶

Sizes: Women's Small (Medium, Large)

To fit shoe sizes: 5–6 (7–9, 10–11)*

*Due to the flexibility of the lacework, the main difference between the sizes is the length of the foot. If you have a narrow foot, use size 0 (2 mm) needles; this will tighten the lace stitches a bit. If your foot is wide, use size 2 (2.75 mm) needles; this will open up the lace stitches a bit.

MATERIALS

2 skeins of Panda Silk from Crystal Palace Yarns (52% bamboo, 43% superwash merino wool, 5% combed silk; 50 g; 204 yds/188 m) in color 4010 (**1**)

2 size 1 (2.25 mm) circular needles (16" and 24")

Point protectors

1 stitch marker

2 stitch holders

Tapestry needle

GAUGE

8 sts = 1" in St st

Avoiding Markers in Lace

The 16" needle (row 1) marks beg of rnd because a stitch marker will only be in the way of working lace patt smoothly. However, if you feel more comfortable using one, attach lockable marker to cast-on toe of first sock to be worked.

TOES

Referring to "Judy's Magic Cast On" on page 45, CO and set up 20 sts for each sock (10 sts per half).

Basic Rnd

Row 1 (16" needle): Knit even across all sts.

Row 2 (24" needle): Sts on this needle are twisted and need to be knit tbl.

Inc Rnds

Only rnds are shown below. For every rnd, you'll work same instructions on 16" needle and 24" needle. See page 17.

All Sizes

Rnd 1: K1, M1R, knit to last st, M1L, K1. Rep for sock 2. (24 sts per sock)

Rnd 2: Knit even across both socks.

Rnd 3: K1, M1R, knit to last st, M1L, K1. Rep for sock 2. (28 sts per sock)

Rnd 4: Knit even across both socks.

Rep rnds 3 and 4 twice more. (36 sts per sock)

Rnd 9: K1, M1R, knit to last st, M1L, K1. Rep for sock 2. (40 sts per sock)

Rnds 10 and 11: Knit even across both socks.

Small and Medium

Rep rnds 9–11 another 4 times. (56 sts per sock)

Large

Rep rnds 9–11 another 5 times. (60 sts per sock)

All Sizes

Toes should measure approx 1$\frac{7}{8}$ (1$\frac{7}{8}$, 2)" from CO edge.

FOOT

The lace patt is worked on instep sts on 24" needle only. All sts on 16" needle (future heel) are knit even each rnd. Make sure YOs are in place where indicated. After you've finished even-numbered rnds, count sts to verify correct amount on your needles.

Work chart (see page 77) for your size as follows.

All Sizes: Rep rnds 1–48 once.

Small: Rep rnds 1–16 once more (approx 6$\frac{1}{2}$" from tip of toe).

Medium: Rep rnds 1–22 once more (approx 7" from tip of toe).

Large: Rep rnds 1–28 once more (approx 7$\frac{1}{2}$" from tip of toe).

Adjusting Foot Length
If you'd like to adjust foot length, you may add or subtract patt rows. Just make sure you end with knit row (even-numbered row) before you begin gusset inc.

GUSSET INCREASES

The gusset is worked on 16" needle (future heel) only.

Rnd 1

Row 1 (16"): K1, M1L, knit to last st, M1R, K1, rep for sock 2. [30 (30, 32) sts]

Row 2 (24"): Cont in lace patt as est across both socks.

Rnd 2 and all even-numbered rnds: Knit across both needles.

Rnd 3

Row 1: K1, M1L, knit to last st, M1R, K1, rep for sock 2. [32 (32, 34) sts]

Row 2: Cont in lace patt as est across both socks.

Rep rnds 2 and 3 until 4 sts per gusset (8 sts total/per sock) have been inc on 16" needle. End with inc/patt rnd 3. [36 (36, 38) sts per half sock]

SHORT-ROW HEEL

Short-row heel (see page 12) is worked back and forth in rows on 16" needle only. Place point protectors on resting needle before you beg.

Unless otherwise specified, sl all sts pw.

Sock 1

Row 1 (16") (RS): Knit to last st, w&t.

Row 2 (16") (WS): Purl to last st, w&t.

Row 3: Knit to last 2 sts, w&t.

Row 4: Purl to last 2 sts, w&t.

Row 5: Knit to last 3 sts, w&t.

Row 6: Purl to last 3 sts, w&t.

Row 7: Knit to last 4 sts, w&t.

Row 8: Purl to last 4 sts, w&t.

Cont to work w&t patt, wrapping 1 new st in each row until total of 12 sts have been wrapped on both sides. [12 (12, 14) sts rem unwrapped in middle section.] This is first part of short-row heel.

Unwrapping Short Rows

Row 1 (RS):

Small and Medium: (K1, ssk) twice, (K1, K2tog) twice to reach first wrapped st (4 sts have been dec).

Large: (K1, ssk) 3 times, K2tog twice, K1 to reach first wrapped st (6 sts have been dec).

There should be 32 sts rem per half sock on 16" needle.

All sizes: Wyib and RH needle, PU wrap on LH needle by slipping it from bottom up through wrap. Leave wrap sitting on RH needle and knit the st that was wrapped; pass wrap over st and off needle like psso. Next st, w&t (it will now be wrapped twice).

Row 2 (WS): Purl to first wrapped st, with wyif and RH needle, PU wrap on RS (facing away from you) from bottom up. Leave wrap sitting on RH needle and purl the st that was wrapped; pass wrap over st and off needle. Next st, w&t (it will now be wrapped twice).

From now on, you'll PU 2 wraps for each st, work and pass wraps over st and off needle.

Row 3: Knit to first wrapped st, with wyib and RH needle, PU wraps and leave on RH needle; knit the st that was wrapped; pass wraps over st and off needle. Next st, w&t.

Rep rows 2 and 3 until all (double) wrapped sts have been worked, ending with row 2.

Now knit even across heel of sock 1 to last 8 sts and put them on st holder unworked. (24 sts rem)

Sock 2

Slide sock 1 to cable and work short-row heel for sock 2. After short-row heel of sock 2 has been worked (ending with a row 2), turn work so RH side of sock 2 is facing you once again.

LEGS

To work lace patt around legs effortlessly, sts have to be moved and beg of rnd changed.

Moving Stitches

16" needle/sock 2 (RS): Knit across first 8 sts, then place these on st holder, knit across rem 24 sts and with same 16" needle, PU 2 (2, 1) sts in gusset corner (between 16" and 24" needle), do not turn, instead cont with 16" needle and knit first 6 (6, 7) sts from 24" needle. This will feel a bit awkward but it helps if you scoot sts on 24" needle close tog and toward needle tip first. Or you can also sl 6 (6, 7) sts from 24" needle onto st holder or cable needle and then knit them off with 16" needle to make it less awkward.

The heel of sock 2 on 16" needle now has 32 sts again, and needles are parallel to each other once more. Turn. The 24" needle is facing you. Note that before starting short-row heels you should have ended lacework with patt row and are now ready to work knit row across 24" needle.

With 24" needle facing you, knit across rem 22 (22, 23) sts of sock 2, which has now become sock 1 on 24" needle. Cont with same needle tip, PU 2 (2, 1) sts in gusset corner and knit 8 sts from st holder (last 8 sts will end up knitted twice). (32 sts.) Move this sock to cable.

24" needle/sock 2: Next, sl 8 sts from holder onto LH side of 24" needle and knit them. Cont with same needle tip, PU 2 (2, 1) sts (you're at space between 16" and 24" needle) and knit across next 22 (22, 23) sts. (32 sts)

Sl rem 6 (6, 7) sts to st holder, turn work, then sl same 6 (6, 7) sts to LH side of 16" needle, ready to be worked.

16" needle/sock 1: K6 (6, 7) sts, PU 2 (2, 1) sts, and knit across rem 24 sts of sock 1.

16" needle/sock 2: Knit even across all sts. (Last 6 sts will end up knitted twice.) Turn.

Floating Pattern Stitches

At the beg of several rnds of the 16-st rep on chart, K1 is highlighted. These are "Floating Pattern Stitches" because they have to float between the 16" and 24" needles to accommodate the pattern. When you get to a highlighted st, K1 and sl the st on lockable st marker, knit across rem st of sock 1. Rep for sock 1, turn and rep for 16" needle. Turn. In next rnd, leave st on marker and cont with YO, then work in patt to last 2 sts, YO, sl 1 kw, sl 1 pw, sl st from marker pw onto LH tip. Then sl last st from RH tip back to LH tip and work dec. Rep for sock 2 and 16" needle.

Note that from now on, 24" needle marks beg of rnd. Cont with correct rnd in lace pattern as est (you should be ready to work patt row). Work 16-st rep twice across each set of sts until leg measures approx 6" to 7" from end of short-row heel.

CUFFS

Work in K1, P1 or K2, P2 ribbing until cuff measures 1". Cont in St st for at least 10 rows, then BO loosely using sewn BO on page 13.

FALLING LEAVES

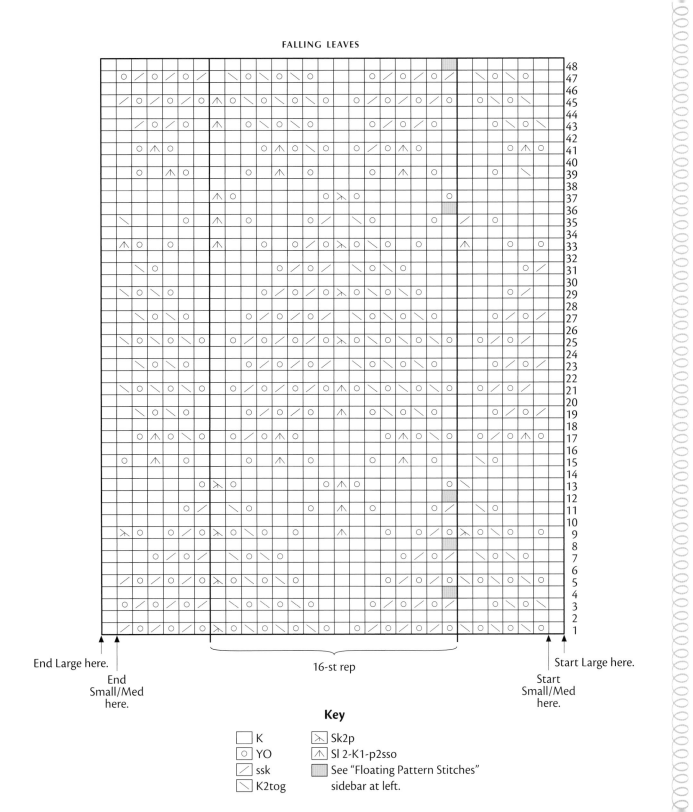

End Large here.

End Small/Med here.

16-st rep

Start Large here.

Start Small/Med here.

Key

☐	K	⋊	Sk2p
⊙	YO	⋀	Sl 2-K1-p2sso
╱	ssk	▨	See "Floating Pattern Stitches"
╲	K2tog		sidebar at left.

Kids' Basic Toe-Up Socks

I love elastic yarns, and have used them in a couple of patterns in this book. The toe-up sock for kids is knitted with Fixation, which by now is gracing the feet of many a knitter. For baby bootees, toddler's socks, and children's socks, this yarn along with other elastic blends is perfect. The socks tend to be soft and spongy, but most importantly, they stay put once slipped on a tiny foot. Equipped with the elastic content, the socks can take whatever children dish out in a day's work. I'm sure you've seen a lonely little sock lost at a playground or in the middle of a sidewalk before. It's a rather sad sight, which can be prevented effortlessly from now on, thanks to elastic yarn. Knit away!

Skill level: Easy ◖■◻◻▷

Sizes: Infant (0–9 mo) [Extra Small (1–2 yrs), Small (3–5 yrs), Medium (6–8 yrs), Large (9–12 yrs)]

To fit shoe sizes: 1–3 (4–6, 7–10, 11–13, 1–4)

MATERIALS

1 (1, 1, 1, 2) skeins of Fixation from Cascade Yarns (98.3% cotton, 1.7% elastic; 50 g; 186 yds stretched/100 yds relaxed) in color 1198 **2**

2 size 5 (3.75 mm) circular needles (16" and 24")

Point protectors

4 stitch markers

Tapestry needle

GAUGE

6 sts = 1" in St st

Highlighting Your Size
Circle or highlight all numbers pertaining to the size socks you are making. That way you won't get confused and accidentally switch sizes while working on your project.

TOES

Referring to "Judy's Magic Cast On" on page 45, CO and set up 12 (12, 12, 16, 16) sts per sock. [6 (6, 6, 8, 8) sts per half] The 16" needle marks beg of rnd.

Basic Rnd

Row 1 (16" needle): Knit even across all sts.

Row 2 (24" needle): All sts on this needle are twisted and need to be knit tbl.

Inc Rnds

Only rnds are shown below. For every rnd, you'll work same instructions on 16" needle and 24" needle. See page 17.

Rnd 1: K1, M1R, knit to last st, M1L, K1. Rep for sock 2. [16 (16, 16, 20, 20) sts per sock]

Rnd 2: Knit even across both socks.

Rnd 3: K1, M1R, knit to last st, M1L, K1. Rep for sock 2. [20 (20, 20, 24, 24) sts per sock]

Rnd 4: Knit even across both socks.

Rep rnds 3 and 4 until there are 32 (32, 32, 36, 40) sts per sock.

Toes should measure approx 1¼ (1¼, 1¼, 1½, 1¾)" from tip.

FOOT

Knit even in rnds until foot measures approx 2 (2¾, 3¼, 4½, 5)" from tip of toe.

EASY HEEL FLAPS

The heel flap is worked back and forth in rows on 16" needle only.

Sl all sts pw unless otherwise specified.

Row 1 (RS): Sl 1 wyif, knit to end. Rep for sock 2.

Row 2 (WS): Sl 1 wyif, purl to last st, K1. Rep for sock 2.

Rep rows 1 and 2 until work measures approx 3½ (4, 4¾, 6¼, 7)" from tip of toe or until heel flap reaches back of heel.

HEEL TURNS

Heel is turned with short rows; therefore each heel is worked separately, beg with sock 1. Cont to work in rows and with same needle as for heel flap. For explanation of italicized instructions in heel turn, see page 16.

Sock 1

All Sizes

Row 1 (RS): Sl 1 wyif, K8 (8, 8, 10, 10) sts, K2tog, K1, turn.

Row 2 (WS): Sl 1 wyif, P3 (3, 3, 5, 3) sts, ssp, P1, turn.

Infant, Extra Small, and Small

Row 3: Sl 1 *kw wyib*, (K1, sl 1) twice, K2tog, K1, turn.

Row 4: Sl 1 wyif, P5, ssp, P1, turn.

Row 5: Sl 1 kw wyib, K2, (sl 1, K1) twice, K2tog, K1, turn.

Row 6: Sl 1 wyif, P7, ssp, P1, turn.

Row 7: Sl 1 *pw wyif*, (K1, sl 1) 4 times, K1, *do not turn*. (10 sts)

Medium

Row 3: Sl 1 *kw wyib*, (K1, sl 1) 3 times, K2tog, K1, turn.

Row 4: Sl 1 wyif, P7, ssp, P1, turn.

Row 5: Sl 1 kw wyib, K2, (sl 1, K1) 3 times, K2tog, K1, turn.

Row 6: Sl 1 wyif, P9, ssp, K1, turn.

Row 7: Sl 1 *pw wyif*, (K1, sl 1) 5 times, K1, *do not turn*. (12 sts)

Large

Row 3: Sl 1 *kw wyib*, (K1, sl 1) twice, K2tog, K1, turn.

Row 4: Sl 1 wyif, P5, ssp, P1, turn.

Row 5: Sl 1 kw wyib, K2, (sl 1, K1) twice, K2tog, K1, turn.

Row 6: Sl 1 wyif, P7, ssp, P1, turn.

Row 7: Sl 1 kw wyib, (K1, sl 1) 4 times, K2tog, K1, turn.

Row 8: Sl 1 wyif, P9, ssp, K1, turn.

Row 9: (K1, sl 1) 6 times, *do not turn*. (12 sts)

All Sizes

Cont with same needle tip, PU 10 (10, 10, 12, 12) sts along side of heel flap, PU 1 gusset st in corner for total of 11 (11, 11, 13, 13) sts.

Sock 2

Move sock to cable and turn heel for sock 2 as for sock 1.

After second heel is turned, cont with **same needle tip**, PU 10 (10, 10, 12, 12) sts along left side of heel flap, PU 1 st in corner for total of 11 (11, 11, 13, 13) sts. Turn. Switch point protectors to appropriate needle. Knit even across instep sts. Turn.

Beg at gusset corner of sock 1, *PU 1 gusset st in corner, PU 10 (10, 10, 12, 12) sts along second side of heel flap for total of 11 (11, 11, 13, 13) sts, pm, knit across all heel sts, place markers, knit across gusset sts on other side. Rep from * for sock 2, beg at gusset corner. Turn. Knit even across all instep sts. Turn.

Both heels are turned and all gusset sts have been picked up. From now on, you'll once again knit in rows as well as rnds. Switch point protectors to tips of resting needle. There are 32 (32, 32, 38, 38) sts on 16" needle and 16 (16, 16, 18, 20) sts on 24" needle.

GUSSET DECREASES

Only heel sts on 16" needle are dec. Sl markers as you get to them.

Infant, Extra Small, and Small

Rnd 1

Row 1 (heel): Knit to first marker, sl 1, (K1, sl 1) 4 times, knit to last 3 sts, K2tog, K1. Rep for sock 2.

Row 2 (instep): Knit even across all sts.

Rnd 2

Row 1: K1, ssk, knit to end. Rep for sock 2.

Row 2: Knit even across all sts.

Medium

Rnd 1

Row 1 (heel): Knit to first marker, sl 1, (K1, sl 1) 5 times, knit to last 3 sts, K2tog, K1. Rep for sock 2.

Row 2 (instep): Knit even across all sts.

Rnd 2

Row 1: K1, ssk, knit to end. Rep for sock 2.

Row 2: Knit even across all sts.

Large

Rnd 1

Row 1 (heel): Knit to first marker, (K1, sl 1) 6 times, knit to last 3 sts, K2tog, K1. Rep for sock 2.

Row 2 (instep): Knit even across all sts.

Rnd 2

Row 1: K1, ssk, knit to end. Rep for sock 2.

Row 2: Knit even across all sts.

All Sizes

Rep rnds 1 and 2 for your size until 16 (16, 16, 18, 20) heel sts rem per sock, matching number of instep sts for total of 32 (32, 32, 36, 40) sts per sock.

Perfect Gusset Triangle (optional): See page 16. Dec as follows, removing markers as you come to them.

Row 1 (heel): K1, ssk, K2, M1L, knit to last 5 sts, M1R, K2, K2tog, K1. Rep for sock 2.

Row 2 (instep): Knit even across both socks.

LEGS

Cont to knit even in rnds until leg measures 1½ (2½, 3, 4¼, 5½)" or until desired length.

CUFFS

Work in K1, P1 or K2, P2 ribbing for 1 to 1½". BO loosely using sewn BO on page 13.

Bjorn's Manly Herringbone Socks

If you want to use at least one extraordinary hand-painted yarn in your sock-knitting career, try Merino Superwash Donegal Tweed from Hand Painted Knitting Yarns. It is one of my all-time favorites! It's soft (very important) and comes in amazingly vibrant color combinations that are all named after operas. It knits up great and washes nicely, but what makes it unique is the Donegal tweed, little tufts of effervescent color that cling to the core, adding a little spice (my favorite).

I once had the pleasure of meeting Rex and Bjorn, the team behind this lovely yarn, and they are just fabulous! Here's to you guys, and to many more skeins of wonderful sock yarn.

Skill level: Intermediate ◖■■■▢

Sizes: Men's Small (Medium, Large, Extra Large)
To fit shoe sizes: 8–9 (10–11, 12–13, 14–15)

MATERIALS

1 skein of Sock Merino Superwash from Hand Painted Knitting Yarns (65% superwash wool, 25% nylon, 10% Donegal; 100 g/3.5 oz; 463 yds) in color Nabucco (**1**)

2 size 1 (2.25 mm) circular needles (16" and 24")

Point protectors

4 stitch markers

Tapestry needle

GAUGE

8 sts = 1" in St st

HERRINGBONE PATTERN

K1B: From the top and front to back, insert RH needle into back of st below next st on LH needle and knit it—1 st inc.

Rnd 1: Knit even across both needles.

Rnd 2: *K2tog, K2, K1B and then knit st above, K2, rep from * across. Rep for sock 2.

Rnd 3: Knit even across both needles.

Rnd 4: *K2, K1B and then knit st above, K2, K2tog, rep from * across. Rep for sock 2.

Rep rnds 1–4.

TOES

Referring to "Judy's Magic Cast On" on page 45, CO and set up 30 sts per sock (15 sts per half). The 16" needle marks beg of rnd.

Basic Rnd

Row 1 (16" needle): Knit even across all sts.

Row 2 (24" needle): All sts on this needle are twisted and need to be knit tbl.

Inc Rnds

Only rnds are shown below. For every rnd, you'll work same instructions on 16" needle and 24" needle. See page 17.

All Sizes

Rnd 1: K1, M1R, knit to last st, M1L, K1. Rep for sock 2. (34 sts per sock)

Rnd 2: Knit even across both socks.

Rnd 3: K1, M1R, knit to last st, M1L, K1. Rep for sock 2. (38 sts per sock)

Rnd 4: Knit even across both socks.

Rep rnds 3 and 4 another 4 times. (54 sts per sock)

Rnds 13 and 14: Knit even across both socks.

Rnd 15: K1, M1R, knit to last st, M1L, K1. Rep for sock 2. (58 sts per sock)

Small and Medium

Rep rnds 13–15 once. (62 sts per sock)

Large and Extra Large

Rep rnds 13–15 another 3 times. (70 sts per sock)

All Sizes

Knit even across both needles for 2 rnds.

Small and Medium

Knit even across both needles for rnd 1 and AT SAME TIME dec 3 sts per sock in row 2 on 24" needle only; 28 sts rem. There are 28 sts on 24" needle and 31 sts on 16" needle.

All Sizes

There are 31 (31, 35, 35) heel sts per sock.

Toes should measure approx 2 (2, 2¼, 2¼)".

FOOT

Herringbone patt is worked on instep sts on 24" needle only. The heel sts on 16" needle are worked in St st (knit all rnds).

Work rnds 1–4 of Herringbone patt until foot measures approx 7¾ (8¼, 8½, 9)" from tip of toe, ending with either rnd 2 or rnd 4.

EASY HEEL FLAPS

The heel flap is worked back and forth in rows on 16" needle only.

Unless otherwise specified, sl all sts pw.

Row 1 (RS): Sl 1 wyif, knit to last 3 sts, K2tog, K1. Rep for sock 2. [30 (30, 34, 34) sts]

Row 2 (WS): Sl 1 wyif, purl to last st, K1. Rep for sock 2.

Row 3 (RS): Sl 1 wyif, knit to end. Rep for sock 2.

Rep rows 2 and 3 until work measures approx 9¾ (10½, 10¾, 11)" from tip of toe or until heel flap reaches back of heel, ending with row 2.

HEEL TURNS

Heel is turned with short rows; therefore, each heel is worked separately, beg with sock 1. Cont to work in rows and with same needle as for heel flap. For explanation of italicized instructions in heel turn, see page 16.

Sock 1

All Sizes

Row 1 (RS): Sl 1 wyif, K16 (16, 18, 18), K2tog, K1, turn.

Row 2 (WS): Sl 1 wyif, P5 ssp, P1, turn.

Row 3: Sl 1 *kw wyib*, (K1, sl 1) 3 times, K2tog, K1, turn.

Row 4: Sl 1 wyif, P7, ssp, P1, turn.

Row 5: Sl 1 kw wyib, K2, (sl 1, K1) 3 times, K2tog, K1, turn.

Row 6: Sl 1 wyif, P9, ssp, P1, turn.

Row 7: Sl 1 kw wyib, (K1, sl 1) 5 times, K2tog, K1, turn.

Row 8: Sl 1 wyif, P11, ssp, P1, turn.

Row 9: Sl 1 kw wyif, K2, (sl 1, K1) 5 times, K2tog, K1, turn.

Row 10: Sl 1 wyif, P13, ssp, P1, turn.

Row 11: Sl 1 kw wyif, (K1, sl 1) 7 times, K2tog, K1, turn.

Small and Medium

Row 12: Sl 1 wyif, P15, ssp, K1, turn.

Row 13: (K1, sl 1) 9 times, *do not turn*. (18 sts rem)

Large and Extra Large

Row 12: Sl 1 wyif, P15, ssp, P1 turn.

Row 13: Sl 1 kw wyib, K2, (K1, sl 1) 7 times, K2tog, K1, turn.

Row 14: Sl 1 wyif, P17, ssp, K1, turn.

Row 15: (K1, sl 1) 10 times, *do not turn.* (20 sts rem)

All Sizes

Cont with same needle tip, PU 16 (17, 18, 19) sts along side of heel flap, PU 1 more st in gusset corner, for total of 17 (18, 19, 20) sts.

Sock 2

Move sock 1 to cable and turn heel for sock 2 same as sock 1. After second heel is turned, cont with same needle tip, PU 16 (17, 18, 19) sts along heel flap, PU 1 gusset st in corner for total of 17 (18, 19, 20) sts Turn. Switch point protectors to appropriate needle.

Cont in Herringbone patt as est and work across both socks on 24" needle. Turn.

Beg at gusset corner of first sock, *PU 1 gusset st in corner, then PU 16 (17, 18, 19) sts along second side of heel flap for total of 17 (18, 19, 20) sts, pm, knit even across 18 (18, 20, 20) heel sts, pm, knit across gusset sts on other side. Rep from * for sock 2, beg in gusset corner. Turn. Work in Herringbone patt as est across both socks on 24" needle.

Both heels are turned and all gusset sts have been picked up. From now on, you'll once again knit in rows as well as rnds. If you still need help remembering, cont to switch point protectors to tips of resting needle. There are 52 (54, 58, 60) sts on 16" needle and 28 (28, 35, 35) sts on 24" needle.

GUSSET DECREASES

Only heel sts are dec. Sl all markers as you get to them.

Rnd 1

Row 1 (heel): Knit to first marker, (K1, sl 1) 9 (9, 10, 10) times, knit to last 3 sts, K2tog, K1. Rep for sock 2.

Row 2 (instep): Work Herringbone patt as est across both socks.

Rnd 2

Row 1 (heel): K1, ssk, knit even to end. Rep for sock 2.

Row 2 (instep): Work Herringbone patt as est across both socks.

Rep rnds 1 and 2 until 30 (30, 34, 34) heel sts are left per sock. Added to 28 (28, 35, 35) instep sts, the total is now 58 (58, 69, 69) sts per sock.

Perfect Gusset Triangle (optional): See page 16. Dec as follows, removing markers as you come to them.

Row 1 (heel): K1, ssk, knit to marker, M1L, knit to next marker, M1R, knit to last 3 sts, K2tog, K1. Rep for sock 2.

Row 2 (instep): Knit even across both socks.

LEGS

Inc Rnd

All sizes

Row 1 (16"/heel): Knit across sts and inc 5 (5, 1, 1) sts evenly per sock. [35 heel sts for all sizes, and total of 63 (63, 70, 70) sts per sock]

The 24" needle marks beg of rnd from now on. Work across all instep sts, turn and cont in patt as est across all sts on 16" needle. Work rnds 1–4 of Herringbone patt across both needles until leg measures approx 6 (6½, 7, 7½)" or until desired length.

CUFFS

Small and Medium
Beg ribbing with a K2tog to even out total sts per sock.

All Sizes
Work in K1, P1 ribbing for 1½". BO loosely using sewn BO on page 13.

The Manly Aran

Many men love handknit socks! But unless they knit themselves, they'll become quite confused when confronted with sock knitting for the first time. "Honey," they interject gently when we come home from the yarn shop all excited and ready to show and tell, "wouldn't it be much cheaper and easier to go to the store and buy a pair of socks?"

Of course it would! But rather than trying to explain, I got my hands on a gorgeous skein of Cascade's new sock yarn, Heritage. I picked one with hues of deep red and a hint of midnight blue, a manly color with a little kick, and made a pair for my husband. As I said before, men love hand-knitted socks . . . as soon as they put them on. Then they ask rather sheepishly when the next pair will be ready for them to wear.

Skill level: Intermediate ■■■□

Sizes: Men's Small (Medium, Large, Extra Large)

To fit shoe sizes: 8–9 (10–11, 12–13, 14–15)

MATERIALS

1 (1, 1, 2) skein of Heritage Hand-Painted Sock Yarn from Cascade Yarns (75% superwash merino wool, 25% nylon; 100 g/3.5 oz; 437 yds/400 m) in color 9926 **1**

Small, Medium, and Large: 2 size 2 (2.75 mm) circular needles (16" and 24")

Extra Large: 2 size 3 (3.25 mm) circular needles (16" and 24")

Point protectors

4 stitch markers

Tapestry needle

GAUGE

Small, Medium, and Large: 8 sts = 1" in St st on size 2 needles

Extra Large: 7½ sts = 1" in St st on size 3 needles

TOES

Referring to "Judy's Magic Cast On" on page 45, CO and set up 24 sts per sock (12 sts per half). The 16" needle marks beg of rnd.

Basic Rnd

Row 1 (16"): Knit even across all sts.

Row 2 (24"): All sts on this needle are twisted and need to be knit tbl.

Inc Rnds

Only rnds are shown below. For every rnd, you'll work same instructions on 16" needle and 24" needle. See page 17.

Rnd 1: K1, M1R, knit to last st, M1L, K1. Rep for sock 2. (28 sts per sock)

Rnd 2: Knit even across both socks.

Rnd 3: K1, M1R, knit to last st, M1L, K1. Rep for sock 2. (32 sts per sock)

Rnd 4: Knit even across both socks.

Rep rnds 3 and 4 another 4 times and rnd 3 once more (52 sts per sock)

Rnds 14 and 15: Knit even across both socks.

Rnd 16: K1, M1R, knit to last st, M1L, K1. Rep for sock 2. (56 sts per sock)

Rnds 17 and 18: Knit even across both socks.

Small

Rnd 19: K1, M1R, knit to last st, M1L, K1. Rep for sock 2. (60 sts per sock)

Medium, Large, and Extra Large

Rnd 19: K1, M1R, knit to last st, M1L, K1. Rep for sock 2. (60 sts per sock)

Rnds 20–22: Knit even across both socks.

Rnd 23: K1, M1R, knit to last st, M1L, K1. Rep for sock 2. (64 sts per sock)

All Sizes

Toes should measure approx 2 (2¼, 2¼, 2½)" from tip.

Knit 1 rnd even across both needles.

FOOT

The Aran patt is worked on 30 (32, 32, 32) instep sts on 24" needle. The heel sts on 16" needle are worked in St st (knit all rnds).

Work chart until foot measures approx 7¾ (8¼, 8½, 9)" from tip of toe.

EASY HEEL FLAPS

The heel flap is worked back and forth in rows on 16" needle only.

Unless otherwise specified, sl all sts pw.

Row 1 (RS): Sl 1 wyif, knit to end. Rep for sock 2.

Row 2 (WS): Sl 1 wyif, purl to last st, K1. Rep for sock 2.

Rep rows 1 and 2 until work measures approx 9¾ (10½, 10¾, 11)" from tip of toe, or until heel flap reaches the back of heel.

HEEL TURNS

The heel is turned with short rows; therefore, each heel is worked separately, beg with sock 1. Cont to work in rows and with same needle as for heel flap. For explanation of italicized instructions in heel turn, see page 16.

Sock 1

All Sizes

Row 1 (RS): Sl 1 wyif, K16, K2tog, K1, turn.

Row 2 (WS): Sl 1 wyif, P5 (3, 3, 3), ssp, P1, turn.

Small

Row 3: Sl 1 *kw wyib*, (K1, sl 1) 3 times, K2tog, K1, turn.

Row 4: Sl 1 wyif, P7, ssp, P1, turn.

Row 5: Sl 1 kw wyib, K2, (sl 1, K1) 3 times, K2tog, K1, turn.

Row 6: Sl 1 wyif, P9, ssp, P1, turn.

Row 7: Sl 1 kw wyib, (K1, sl 1) 5 times, K2tog, K1, turn.

Row 8: Sl 1 wyif, P11, ssp, P1, turn.

Row 9: Sl 1 kw wyif, K2, (sl 1, K1) 5 times, K2tog, K1, turn.

Row 10: Sl 1 wyif, P13, ssp, P1, turn.

Row 11: Sl 1 kw wyif, (K1, sl 1) 7 times, K2tog, K1, turn.

Row 12: Sl 1 wyif, P15, ssp, K1, turn.

Row 13: (K1, sl 1) 9 times, *do not turn.* (18 sts)

Medium, Large, and Extra Large

Row 3: Sl 1 *kw wyib*, (K1, sl 1) twice, K2tog, K1, turn.

Row 4: Sl 1 wyif, P5, ssp, P1, turn.

Row 5: Sl 1 kw wyib, K2, (sl 1, K1) twice, K2tog, K1, turn.

Row 6: Sl 1 wyif, P7, ssp, P1, turn.

Row 7: Sl 1 kw wyib, (K1, sl 1) 4 times, K2tog, K1, turn.

Row 8: Sl 1 wyif, P9, ssp, P1, turn.

Row 9: Sl 1 kw wyif, K2, (sl 1, K1) 4 times, K2tog, K1, turn.

Row 10: Sl 1 wyif, P11, ssp, P1, turn.

Row 11: Sl 1 kw wyif, (K1, sl 1) 6 times, K2tog, K1, turn.

Row 12: Sl 1 wyif, P13, ssp, P1 turn.

Row 13: Sl 1 kw wyib, K2, (sl 1, K1) 6 times, K2tog, K1, turn.

Row 14: Sl 1 wyif, P15, ssp, K1, turn.

Row 15: (K1, sl 1) 9 times, *do not turn*. (18 sts)

All Sizes

Cont with same needle tip, PU 16 (17, 18, 19) sts along side of heel flap, PU 1 more st in gusset corner for total of 17 (18, 19, 20) sts.

Sock 2

Move first sock to cable and turn heel for sock 2 same as sock 1. After second heel is turned, cont with same needle tip, PU 16 (17, 18, 19) sts along heel flap, PU 1 gusset st in corner for total of 17 (18, 19, 20) sts. Turn. Switch point protectors to appropriate needle.

Cont in Aran patt as est and work across both socks on 24" needle. Turn.

Beg at gusset corner of first sock, *PU 1 gusset st in corner, then PU 16 (17, 18, 19) sts along second side of heel flap for total of 17 (18, 19, 20) sts, pm, knit even across 18 heel sts, pm, knit across gusset sts on other side. Rep from * for sock 2, beg in gusset corner. Turn.

Work in Aran patt as est across both socks on 24" needle.

Both heels are turned and all gusset sts have been picked up. From now on, you'll once again knit in rows as well as rnds. Cont to switch point protectors to tips of resting needle. There are 52 (54, 56, 58) sts on 16" needle and 30 (32, 32, 32) sts on 24" needle.

GUSSET DECREASES

Only heel sts are dec. Sl all markers as you get to them.

Rnd 1

Row 1 (heel): Knit to first marker, (K1, sl 1) 9 times, knit to last 3 sts, K2tog, K1. Rep for sock 2.

Row 2 (instep): Work Aran patt as est across both socks.

Rnd 2

Row 1 (heel): K1, ssk, knit even to end. Rep for sock 2.

Row 2 (instep): Work Aran patt as est across both socks.

Rep rnds 1 and 2 until 30 (32, 32, 32) heel sts are left per sock, matching number of instep sts for total of 60 (64, 64, 64) sts per sock.

Perfect Gusset Triangle (optional): See page 16. Dec as follows, removing markers as you come to them.

Row 1 (heel): K1, ssk, knit to marker, M1L, knit to next marker, M1R, knit to last 3 sts, K2tog, K1. Rep for sock 2.

Row 2 (instep): Knit even across both socks.

LEGS

Beg Aran patt with correct row to match est instep patt. Cont to work in rnds, following chart until leg measures 6 (7, 7½, 7½)" or until desired length.

CUFFS

Work in K2, P2 ribbing for 1½" or until desired length. BO loosely using sewn BO on page 13.

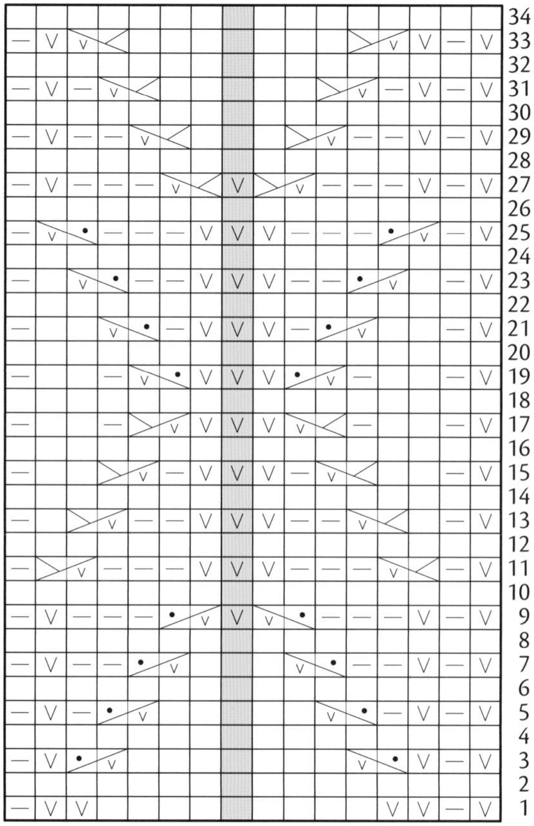

Key

- K
- P
- K1 tbl
- Sl 1 st on cn and hold in back, K1 tbl, K1 from cn.
- Sl 1 st to cn and hold in back, K1 tbl, P1 from cn.
- Sl 1 st on cn and hold in front, K1, K1 tbl from cn.
- Sl 1 st to cn and hold in front, P1, K1 tbl from cn.
- Do not work for size Small.

Converting Patterns
From Double-Pointed to Circular Needles

Once you've become comfortable with the basic pattern, you'll be able to convert any sock pattern from double-pointed needles to two circular needles. Conventional sock patterns use either three or four double-pointed needles to set up the sock. For clarification, the needles are numbered and carry specific stitches—for example, the instep or part of the heel. Whatever the case may be, when using two circular needles, the stitches are simply divided in half with one needle carrying all the instep stitches and the other carrying all the heel or sole stitches.

In traditional sock patterns, knitters have to work with multiple needles, remember which needle corresponds to which number of stitches, and can only work on one sock at a time. The cuff and leg are worked in the round for so many inches. Then the real fun begins. For the heel flap and turning of the heel, knitters have to remember which number of stitches belongs to which needle and switch stitches from one needle to another ("M1, sl 1, dec 1") until finally all heel stitches are sitting on one needle. But it doesn't stop there; once finished with the heel, stitches have to get moved and shifted again to accommodate the gusset, which is worked on two needles (but which ones?).

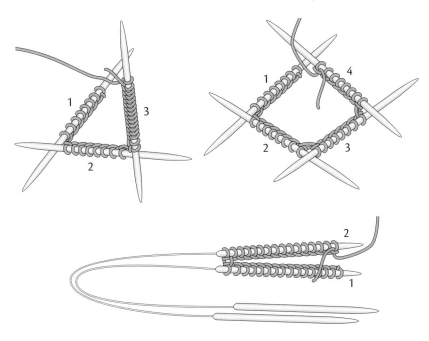

Using circular needles utterly simplifies sock knitting. Look at the traditional pattern you've picked to convert.

1. Cast on and set up X amount of sts on your two circular needles.

2. Work cuff and leg in the round to desired length.

3. Work heel flap (sitting on one circular needle) back and forth using traditional pattern to the desired length.

4. Ignore all shifting of stitches in the traditional pattern and go straight to heel-turning instructions. Since the heel is turned on one needle, regardless of how many double-pointed needles are indicated, turn your heel exactly as described in the pattern, using the circular needle that holds the heel flap.

5. Once the heel is turned, ignore all shifting of stitches in the traditional pattern and simply find the amount of stitches to be picked up for the gusset. Then follow the circular needle instructions and pick up all gusset stitches plus the extra corner stitches.

6. From now on, you can ignore the traditional pattern altogether and follow the circular pattern to decrease the gusset stitches back to the original stitch count. Then work the foot.

7. For the toe, you can choose one of the decreases in this book, decrease every other round, or use the gradual decrease for a more rounded effect; or, you can use the decrease in the traditional pattern. Remember that all decreases always take place in one round and at both sides of both circular needles.

8. Check the traditional pattern to see how many toe stitches are left before it's closed with the Kitchener stitch, and decrease accordingly.

Once you've converted a few patterns, you'll get used to quickly gathering all the necessary information needed from the traditional pattern and transferring it to your circular needles.

Abbreviations and Glossary

approx .... approximately
beg .... begin(ning)
BO .... bind off
CC .... contrasting color
cn .... cable needle
CO .... cast on
cont .... continue(ing)
dec .... decrease(s)(ing)
EOR .... every other row
est .... established
g .... gram(s)
inc .... increase(s)(ing)
K .... knit
K1B .... Knit 1 below increase (see page 83)
K2tog .... knit 2 stitches together (see page 10)
K3tog .... knit 3 stitches together
kw .... knitwise
LH .... left hand
M1L .... make 1 stitch/left-slanted (see page 11)
M1R .... make 1 stitch/right-slanted (see page 11)
MC .... main color
mm .... millimeters
mos .... months
oz .... ounces
P .... purl
patt .... pattern
pm .... place marker

psso .... pass slipped stitch over
PU .... pick up and knit
pw .... purlwise
rem .... remain(ing)
rep(s) .... repeat(s)
RH .... right hand
rnd(s) .... round(s)
RS .... right side
sk2p .... slip 1, K2tog, pass slipped stitch over the K2tog (see page 11)
sl .... slip
sl 2-K1-p2sso ...... slip 2 knitwise, K1, pass 2 slipped stitches over knit stitch (see page 11)
sl st .... slip stitch
ssk .... slip, slip, knit (see page 10)
ssp .... slip, slip, purl (see page 10)
st(s) .... stitch(es)
St st .... stockinette stitch
tbl .... through back loop
w&t .... wrap and turn (see page 12)
wyib .... with yarn in back
wyif .... with yarn in front
WS .... wrong side
yds .... yards
yrs .... years
YO .... yarn over

USEFUL INFORMATION

YARN-WEIGHT SYMBOLS						
Yarn-Weight Symbol and Category Names	**1** Super Fine	**2** Fine	**3** Light	**4** Medium	**5** Bulky	**6** Super Bulky
Type of Yarns in Category	Sock, Fingering, Baby	Sport, Baby	DK, Light Worsted	Worsted, Afghan, Aran	Chunky, Craft, Rug	Bulky, Roving
Knit Gauge in Stockinette Stitch to 4"	27 to 32 sts	23 to 26 sts	21 to 24 sts	16 to 20 sts	12 to 15 sts	6 to 11 sts
Recommended Needle in U.S. Size	1 to 3	3 to 5	5 to 7	7 to 9	9 to 11	11 and larger
Recommended Needle in Metric Size	2.25 to 3.25 mm	3.25 to 3.75 mm	3.75 to 4.5 mm	4.5 to 5.5 mm	5.5 to 8 mm	8 mm and larger

SKILL LEVELS

■□□□ **Beginner:** Projects for first-time knitters using basic knit and purl stitches. Minimal shaping.

■■□□ **Easy:** Project using basic stitches, repetitive stitch patterns, and simple color changes. Simple shaping and finishing.

■■■□ **Intermediate:** Projects using a variety of stitches, such as basic cables and lace, simple intarsia, and techniques for double-pointed needles and knitting in the round. Midlevel shaping.

■■■■ **Experienced:** Projects using advanced techniques and stitches, such as short rows, Fair Isle, more intricate intarsia, cables, lace patterns, and numerous color changes.

METRIC CONVERSIONS

Yards x .91 = meters

Meters x 1.09 = yards

Grams x .0352 = ounces

Ounces x 28.35 = grams

Yarn Sources

Contact the following companies to locate shops that carry the yarns featured in this book.

Blue Ridge Yarns
www.mistymountainfarm.com
Jubilee

Cascade Yarns
www.cascadeyarns.com
Cascade 220 Tweed
Fixation
Heritage Hand-Painted Sock Yarn

Conjoined Creations
www.conjoinedcreations.com
Flat Feet

Crystal Palace Yarns
www.straw.com
Maizy
Panda Silk

Dream in Color
www.dreamincoloryarn.com
Classy

Hand Painted Knitting Yarns
www.handpaintedknittingyarns.com
Sock Merino Superwash

Louet
www.louet.com
Gems Super Fine Fingering Weight

Tahki Stacy Charles
Filatura Di Crosa
www.tahkistacycharles.com
Maxime Print

The Alpaca Yarn Company
www.thealpacayarnco.com
Paca Peds Superwash Alpaca Sock Yarn

KNITTING AND CROCHET TITLES

ACCESSORIES
Crocheted Pursenalities
Crocheted Socks!
Kitty Knits
Pursenalities
Pursenality Plus
Stitch Style: Mittens
Toe-Up Techniques for Hand-Knit Socks,
Revised Edition

BABIES, CHILDREN, & TOYS
Gigi Knits…and Purls
Knitted Finger Puppets
Knitting with Gigi
Too Cute!

CROCHET
365 Crochet Stitches a Year: Perpetual Calendar
Amigurumi World
A to Z of Crochet
Contemporary Crochet—*NEW!*
First Crochet

LITTLE BOX SERIES
The Little Box of Crocheted Gifts
The Little Box of Crocheted Throws
The Little Box of Knitted Gifts
The Little Box of Knitted Throws
The Little Box of Socks

KNITTING
200 Knitted Blocks
365 Knitting Stitches a Year: Perpetual Calendar
All about Knitting
A to Z of Knitting
Beyond Wool
Cable Confidence
Casual, Elegant Knits
Chic Knits
Fair Isle Sweaters Simplified
Handknit Skirts
Knit One, Stripe Too
The Knitter's Book of Finishing Techniques
Ocean Breezes
Simple Gifts for Dog Lovers
Simple Stitches
Skein for Skein
Special Little Knits from Just One Skein
Stripes, Stripes, Stripes
Together or Separate
Top Down Sweaters
Wrapped in Comfort

SOCK KNITTING
Knitting Circles around Socks
More Sensational Knitted Socks
Sensational Knitted Socks
Stitch Style: Socks

Our books are available at bookstores and your favorite craft, fabric, and yarn retailers. If you don't see the title you're looking for, visit us at **www.martingale-pub.com** or contact us at:
1-800-426-3126
International: 1-425-483-3313
Fax: 1-425-486-7596 • **Email:** info@martingale-pub.com

Martingale®
& COMPANY

America's Best-Loved Craft & Hobby Books®
America's Best-Loved Knitting Books®

3/09 Knit